Bartolomé de las Casas
AND THE
Defense of Amerindian Rights

Atlantic Crossings
Gabriel Paquette, Series Editor

Bartolomé de las Casas
AND THE
Defense of Amerindian Rights

A Brief History with Documents

EDITED BY
LAWRENCE A. CLAYTON
and
DAVID M. LANTIGUA

THE UNIVERSITY OF ALABAMA PRESS
Tuscaloosa

The University of Alabama Press
Tuscaloosa, Alabama 35487-0380
uapress.ua.edu

Inquiries about reproducing material from this work should be addressed to the
University of Alabama Press.

Typeface: Caslon

Cover image: Detail from a Cuban postage stamp, c. 1944, depicting
"Bartolome de las Casas, Defensor de Los Indios, 1492–1942"
Cover design: David Nees

Cataloging-in-Publication data is available from the Library of Congress.
ISBN: 978-0-8173-5969-0
E-ISBN: 978-0-8173-9285-7

For David's loving parents, Carlos and Myriam Lantigua

Contents

Illustrations follow page 63.

Acknowledgments

Many contributed to this book in various ways, from inspiration to helping us bring the work to fruition. In particular, there would have been little opportunity to develop this book together were it not for David Orique, OP, who first introduced us to each other at a 2011 conference hosted by Alma College commemorating Antonio Montesinos, OP, and the first Dominican preachers in the New World. In addition, this book has been made possible in part by support from the Institute for Scholarship in the Liberal Arts, College of Arts and Letters, at the University of Notre Dame.

We would personally like to thank our editor at the University of Alabama Press, Dan Waterman, a consummate professional who never let details and demands get in the way of his care for both us and the book. We also benefitted from readings and suggestions made by Bonnie Smith at Rutgers University on an earlier version of the manuscript. The Strake Foundation through The Catholic University of America generously assisted in providing for the research materials used in some of the translations of this book. The Department of Theology, as well as the Institute for Latino Studies, both at the University of Notre Dame, also provided David with research leave to complete this book, for which we are especially grateful. Others who have contributed to the completion of this book over its long development include José Cárdenas Bunsen, Daniel Brunstetter, Thomas Cohen, Fr. Mark Morozowich, Matthew Ashley, Luis G. Rey, Timothy Matovina, and Luis Fraga.

Finally, this book would never have been completed without the abiding love and support from family. David would like to thank his wife, Marisa, the benevolent source for the perseverance required to complete this project with grace, joy, and patience. Her loving care for their children, Sofia, Natalia, Elena, and Lilia, each of whom is a blessing beyond measure, has been his greatest daily inspiration. David is especially grateful for his parents, Carlos and Myriam Lantigua, whose gifts of faith and sacrificial love have moved many, many mountains. He dedicates this book to them and our shared Hispanic heritage, to which Larry adds a loud "amen," and an equally deep and abiding thanks to wife, Louise, for her patience and support of her husband's long friendship and admiration for a friar who lived centuries ago but who still inspires us all today.

Bartolomé de las Casas

AND THE

Defense of Amerindian Rights

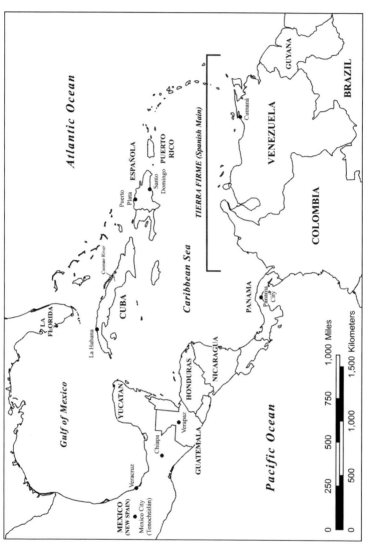

Map 1. Las Casas traveled and worked in his defense of the American Indians in Cuba, Haiti, Dominican Republic, Puerto Rico, Venezuela, Panama, Nicaragua, Honduras, Guatemala, and Mexico. Courtesy of the University of Alabama Cartographic Research Lab.

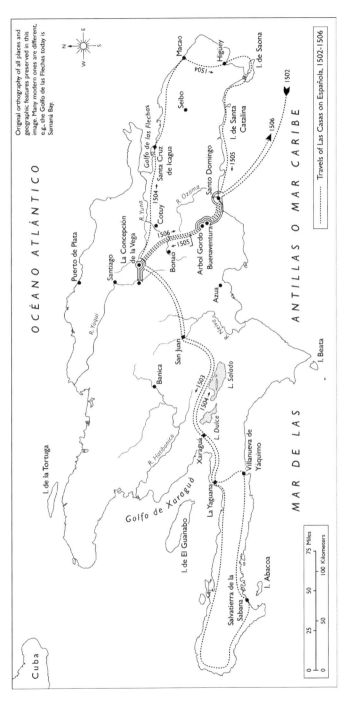

Map 2. The routes of some of Las Casas's travels between 1502, when he first arrived in the Indies, and 1506, around the island of Española (today, Haiti and the Dominican Republic), where he spent much of his early life in the Indies.

Introduction

Bartolomé de las Casas, a larger-than-life cleric and often reviled critic of Spanish treatment of Indians, was born in Seville, Spain, in 1484.[1] After Christopher Columbus, there is no more prominent figure in the Spanish conquest of the Americas than Las Casas. Columbus and the conquistadors who followed him subjugated the native Amerindian peoples, from the islands of the Caribbean to the great complex Aztec (Nahua) and Inca empires of Mexico and Peru.[2] Often assisted by numerous other natives, the Spanish forced and incorporated Amerindians under their sovereignty by using war and enslavement as the chief means. Over the course of his epic life across continents and oceans, Las Casas was someone who uniquely stood on both sides of the conquest as a one-time oppressor and later a defender of the dispossessed peoples of the Americas. He was truly a Renaissance figure inhabiting many roles in life from priest, missionary, and bishop to lawyer, historian, and philosopher. These documents tell his story.

The Conquest of the Americas

In the following pages, both in this introduction and in the documents that follow, you will read about the Spanish forced occupation of the Americas in the late fifteenth and throughout the sixteenth century. To understand Las Casas's place in this relatively short but intense and seminal period in the history of the world, we need some context.

Before 1492, Europeans knew little or nothing of the existence of what we call the Western Hemisphere, or the Americas. And the inhabitants of the Americas knew nothing of the European world, nor of Africa or Asia, for that matter. Columbus's four voyages to the Americas, between 1492 and

1504, established contact between two worlds, which until then had shared little other than the waters and vast expanse of the Atlantic Ocean that washed both the coast of Europe and the shores of the Americas.

Spanish colonization of the Americas began with the very first exploitation of the natives of the islands in the Caribbean that were discovered, explored, and settled by Columbus and other mariners and navigators and soldiers who followed him. The Spanish took advantage of their superiority in arms and fighting, compounded by European diseases, to subjugate the Amerindian peoples by reducing them to forced labor and slavery. The conquests spread over the islands for the next twenty to twenty-five years and then moved onto the mainland of Mexico, Central America, and finally South America by the 1530s. The conquistador class—a term loosely applied to all the navigators, early settlers, soldiers, and others—was driven largely by ambitions for wealth and glory and was capable of cruelty and plundering in hostile situations. Their fighting instincts, boldness in battle, and sureness of themselves had been toughened in the final stages of the Reconquest of Spain. The Reconquest was basically the 500-year struggle between Christian Spain and Moorish (what Islam was called in Spain) Spain for dominance of the Iberian Peninsula. It culminated in 1492 with the capitulation of the last Moorish kingdom of Granada.

The conquest of the Americas that started in 1492–1493 has often been viewed as an extension of the Reconquest and the Crusades before it.[3] In a manner it was. Spanish soldiers were the toughest in Europe and emerged from the Reconquest as proud, experienced, and battle-hardened entrepreneurs. The native Americans on the islands of the Caribbean were, on the other hand, often woefully unprepared by their culture and traditions to resist such a determined invader, and so conquests proceeded, past the islands and onto the mainland of North America, Mexico, Central America, and South America. When the Spaniards encountered large-scale societies like the Aztec empire, they did not do so alone but instead capitalized on subjugated enemy natives by enlisting the latter as Spanish allies in the effort to topple the dominant Amerindian regime in question.[4]

Among the most famous, and successful, of the conquistadors was Hernán Cortés, who subjugated regions of Mexico (called New Spain by the Europeans) between 1519 and 1522, and Francisco Pizarro, who invaded Peru on the west coast of South America in 1532 and in a swift campaign reduced the vast Inca Empire strung out along the coast and mountains of Bolivia, Peru, and Ecuador to obedience by 1534. Inca resistance and rebellions and internecine war among Pizarro's followers turned the Peruvian theater into a chaotic frontier-like drama. But the inevitable consequence of expeditions led by Cortés, Pizarro, and others was the expansion of the Spanish Empire in the New World, or "*el Nuevo Mundo.*"

The conquest was, moreover, a multifaceted phenomenon. It was not simply greedy conquistadors demolishing Indian warriors. It took Cortés and his army and allies two years to subdue the Aztec capital of Tenochtitlan (today's Mexico City), which was defended by tens of thousands of equally determined Aztec warriors. These warriors, in one celebrated campaign, had expelled the invading Spaniards in a battle the Spanish called *la noche triste*, or the sad night, because of the military disaster that befell them. But the inexorable ability of the Spanish to lick their wounds and recover their strength inevitably led to the final crushing of Aztec resistance. By then, European diseases such as smallpox had played an equal role in undermining the will and ability of the Aztecs to prevail in the face of such a determined foe.

Furthermore—and here is where Las Casas begins to appear in our picture—all the earliest Spaniards were Christians, and for some their Catholic faith sustained and lifted them up in various military battles and campaigns. They went into battle with the battle cry *¡Santiago y Matamoros!* or "St. James and Kill Moors," just as they had in the final siege of Granada and the war against the Moors (Muslims). That the natives of the Caribbean islands, or the Aztecs of Mexico or the Incas of Peru, knew nothing of St. James or killing Moors is a given. But to some Spanish warriors, the conquest of the New World was a crusade of sorts. As one famous chronicler who marched with Cortés into Mexico remarked, "We came to serve God and get rich."[5]

Many clerics (a general term for Roman Catholic priests of all ranks), even members of some of the most prominent religious orders, accompanied the explorers and conquistadors. Members of these Catholic religious orders were brothers and priests who had taken special vows such as celibacy and obedience, with lives committed to study, prayer, and service. The two prominent orders—the Franciscans and Dominicans—were also known as mendicants, or "begging friars," named after their respective thirteenth-century medieval founders, St. Francis of Assisi and St. Dominic. These friars took an additional vow of poverty, unlike other clerics, to preach the Gospel. Las Casas, as you will read below, was first ordained as a secular priest but later entered the Dominicans (or the Order of Preachers), so he is often described below as a missionary.

Bartolomé de las Casas

Joined by many other Dominicans and Franciscans, Las Casas challenged the idea and practice of conquest with so much passion and commitment that he emerged as the most notable defender of Amerindians in this unique period of encounter and colonization. Modern Western civilization, for better and for worse, grew out of this fateful encounter between Europeans and native Americans. Las Casas engaged kings and emperors, warriors and priests, popes and the grandees of Spain and Europe as he crisscrossed this Atlantic world and fought for the rights and freedom of Amerindians in the forums of power across Spain and the (West) Indies.

At the time, Spain was triumphantly ending a centuries-long war against the Moorish people of Spain. They had invaded the Iberian Peninsula (modern Spain and Portugal) in 711 AD, coming across the Straits of Gibraltar from Africa and spreading Islam into Europe. They conquered much of the Iberian Peninsula and created a dynamic political and cultural presence in Spain with its capital at the city of Córdoba.

Then about 1000 AD, some small Christian kingdoms in the north of Spain that had survived Islamic expansion, began what became known in Spanish history as the Reconquest. The war between Christianity and Islam sputtered off and on for almost 500 years until the final Muslim kingdom, the Caliphate of Granada in the southeast of Spain, fell early in 1492 to the combined Christian armies and knights of Queen Isabel of Castile and her husband, King Ferdinand of Aragon. That same year, Columbus landed on the islands of the Indies, mistaking them initially as an alternative trade route to Asia. Both worlds of the Reconquest and the Conquest, the old world and the new, fused together in the Spanish popular imagination. One chronicler, who was also Cortés's personal chaplain, captured the zealous and violent spirit of Spain during this period when he wrote: "The conquest of the Indians began once the conquests of the Moors ended, because Spaniards always wage war against infidels."[6]

Las Casas was born into this bellicose Spanish religious world. It was a martial society, prone to war in the name of protecting the faith, fighting over half a millennium for European Christendom. The Spanish legal code of King Alfonso X known as *Las Siete Partidas* (Seven Part-Code), which dated back to the thirteenth century, considered war just when its purpose was to spread the faith and destroy enemies like the Moors.[7] Religious war, or holy war, provided a legal mechanism for acquiring slaves effectively. The Reconquest was not a simple event, however. Christians and Moors weren't always at war; in fact, they oftentimes occupied large portions of Spain in peaceful coexistence. They usually tolerated a small but important segment of their population, the Jews of Spain. Las Casas grew up in this polyglot society of Christians, Jews, and Moors all living side by side but worshipping differently. Overall, Christendom was moving into a period of intense reform, orthodoxy, and growing intolerance precipitated by the Protestant Reformation within Europe and the persistent military strength of Muslims at its borders.

Las Casas's father was a generally well-to-do merchant with numerous contacts and relatives in various communities like the church and among merchants, sailors, and mariners in the port city of Seville. Bartolomé, who joined the church as a priest early in his life, witnessed some extraordinary events as he grew up in Seville. His world was transformed by the burgeoning nationalism and religious intolerance of Isabel and Ferdinand who, by their marriage in 1469, united all the major medieval kingdoms of Spain into a new entity, early modern Spain. While the final surrender of Granada marked the end of the Reconquest and was a turning point in Spanish history, a small fleet of three ships sailed out from the port of Palos on the Andalusian seacoast into the Atlantic Ocean in August of 1492. What they found was as transformative in the history of the modern world as the fall of Granada was for the formation of early modern Spain. This event—the discovery, exploration, and occupation of a new world— transformed Las Casas as well. He was, in fact, at the epicenter of a rapidly changing European world.

Columbus

The fleet of the *Santa Maria*, *Niña*, and *Pinta* was commanded by an Italian-born mariner, Christopher Columbus, in the service of Isabel and Ferdinand. Columbus set out to find a sea route to the Spice Islands of the east, perhaps hit upon Cipangu (China), or even make his way to India. If he could find a sea route to the Holy Land (today's Israel as well as parts of Syria, Palestine, Lebanon, and Egypt), his mission as a Christian—to recapture Jerusalem from Islam—would be celebrated and make him famous.

Instead, as we know, he landed on an island in the Bahamas called San Salvador by Spaniards, and Watlings Island by Englishmen. Asia, including the Spice Islands and China, were thousands of miles far to the west across the vast Pacific Ocean. Columbus explored the Bahamas, stopped at Cuba, and made his way to the north coast of a large island he named Española (anglicized later to Hispaniola and today modern Haiti and the Dominican Republic). He returned to Spain in 1493 and then recruited a large expedition which he commanded in 1494, returning to the islands he had discovered. There were people, the Arawaks and Taínos on Cuba and Hispaniola, respectively, and they had gold. Colonization by conquest had begun.

Seville, March 31, 1493

After returning to Spain from his historic first voyage in 1492–1493, Columbus arrived in Seville on Palm Sunday, March 31, 1493. In his entourage marched seven Taíno Indians captured in the Caribbean. Dressed in their native feathers and fishbone and gold ornaments, they drew curious stares from the gawking onlookers, as much impressed by the parrots as the strange "Indians." Young Las Casas—then about eight years old—witnessed the procession into the city. Did the boy feel compassion for these awkward natives who seemed so out of place in late medieval Seville?

The Admiral had sailed south and west. What had he found? The excitement stirred by Columbus rippled through the land. He continued from Seville on his triumphant trip to Barcelona, where he showed Isabel and Ferdinand the fruits of his voyage of exploration. The Catholic Sovereigns were delighted with the evidence that Providence had dropped in their laps—exotic Indians who needed to be converted to Christianity, gold articles that meant material wealth in this world, and the persuasive Columbus's promise of more, much more (see Documents 1–2). The pope in Rome, Alexander VI, soon thereafter expressed his support for the new imperial venture in a so-called letter of Donation called *Inter caetera*, which granted Spain the title to introduce Christianity to the newly encountered peoples of the Indies.

To the Indies, 1502

As a young man, Las Casas first crossed the Atlantic to the early Spanish settlements on the Caribbean islands in 1502. After assisting as a chaplain in the conquest of Cuba, Las Casas acquired Amerindians who could provide tributary labor and service for the Spanish Crown. The natives now fatefully belonged to the colonial institution called the *encomienda*—introduced by Columbus's Spanish colonists a few years earlier. This new world institution had its feudal roots in the old-world practice of the Reconquest when crusading military orders were granted jurisdiction over taxable land and its subjects by the Crown.[8]

To mine gold and later silver in the newly possessed lands, Amerindians were assigned to *encomenderos* such as Las Casas, who then had the royal duty of instructing them in the faith. The natives were not literally slaves, for the pious and protective Isabel had forbidden the enslavement of her new "subjects." Columbus and the Spaniards originally received instructions from Queen Isabel to treat "the said Indians very well and lovingly."[9] But facts on the ground relate something very different. The difference between slavery and *encomienda* Indians became merely a formality under the forced labor system.[10] For the next ten years, Las Casas was both actor and witness in the destruction of the native Taínos of the island and elsewhere.

"Each Spaniard had an itch for gold and a narrow conscience," he wrote.[11]

"They had no thought that those natives were made of flesh and blood. They put them to work in the [gold] mines and at other projects the Indians could only accomplish as slave labor, put them to work so promptly, so pitilessly that in a few days' time many native deaths showed the brutality of Spanish treatment" (see Document 3). In the eyes of the Spanish, the island natives were a lazy and idle people who had no industry and private possessions. Putting them to work in the mines, however dangerous, would only assuage the conscience of *encomenderos*.

Demoralized, hunted down, and shocked further by European infections to which they had no resistance, the Amerindians of the Caribbean died by the scores, then hundreds, then hundreds of thousands, until by 1520 and 1530, only a handful survived where millions before had lived. This was the very essence of the "Black Legend," so often associated with Las Casas. Las Casas, in fact, is known principally in the English-speaking world as the author of this Black Legend. The legend pillories the Spanish character for its allegedly unique combination of cruelty and insensitivity that characterized the Conquest.

His best-known book, *An Account, Much Abbreviated, of the Destruction of the Indies* (1552), described the atrocities committed by Christian conquistadors on Amerindians of the New World, the very ones he witnessed on Hispaniola. Las Casas gave sorrowful heed to the Requirement (or *Requerimiento*) read aloud to the natives in many of the lands on the American continent, "requiring that they come into the faith and render obedience to the king and queen of Castile, and telling them that if they do not do this, then fiery, bloody war will be waged upon them and they will be slain and captured."[12] The Requirement was a legal ruse combining violent biblical narrative with the fervor of the Reconquest. It allegedly offered a choice to Amerindians between Spanish Christian political subjugation or war and enslavement. Its principal author was the jurist Juan López de Palacios Rubios (1450–1524), who endorsed a policy of converting Amerindians by means of conquest. This legal fiction disturbed Las Casas wholeheartedly until the end of his life.

The island of Hispaniola was "pacified, if 'pacified' we can in truth call it," Las Casas wrote later with bitter sarcasm, "seeing as how the Spaniards were at war with God, free now to oppress these people with great liberty, and nobody, great or small, to resist them."

This was a very fluid period in the relations between Europeans and Amerindians, but by 1503 and 1504, Las Casas knew in his heart that this emerging order was all wrong. He was shocked at the brutal callousness of the Spaniards. Persecuting heretics and catapulting Moorish body parts into besieged cities during the final campaign for the Reconquest of the Moorish kingdom of Granada may have been common fare at home, but these innocent people were not apostates and heretics.[13]

Later, Las Casas recorded everything he had witnessed in a torrent of writing for sixty years until his death in 1566. He was on his way to becoming the greatest European defender of Amerindian freedom during the sixteenth century. He left an immense body of writing, testifying to his multiple roles of chronicler, historian, theologian, bishop, lawyer, activist, and reformer.

To defend the natives, Las Casas drew heavily from the principal theological doctrines of Christianity that emphasized love and equality and recognition of everyone as "born and raised up in the image of God."[14] In his advocacy for them, he indicted his fellow countrymen—the Spaniards and so-called Christians—for their callous, self-centered, rapacious behavior. He became, in fact, the conscience of the Conquest, the very antithesis of the conquistador, and, in doing so, Las Casas lay the basis for the modern human rights movement, certainly in Latin America.[15]

He remained in Hispaniola until 1511, when he was invited to join an expedition to the neighboring island of Cuba (see Document 4). Although growing in his criticism of Spanish settlers and their exploitation of the Taínos, he had not yet quite turned the page into the ardent critic he became. His participation in the invasion and "pacification"—a cynical synonym for the conquest—of the Taíno people of Cuba culminated in witnessing a massacre of Arawaks along the River Caonao in central Cuba. His outrage as a human being and his Christian conscience were both seared by the slaughter of hundreds of innocents by Spanish soldiers and cavalry.

Caonao was his epiphany, the moment he realized he could no longer condone the conquests. He returned to Spain late in 1515 to petition King Ferdinand, who was close to death, to rectify these terrible wrongs. Even worse was the excuse used by the Spaniards. They had to use force to convert the Amerindians to the one true faith. It was hypocrisy of the worst sort, hellishly condemning the violent Spaniards by their own religious standards. Las Casas reiterated this point loudly and frequently.

Las Casas subsequently emerged at the center of perhaps the greatest controversy and challenge in the history of Western man—how to incorporate a "new" world, and a "new" people, the Amerindians—into the context of European culture and civilization in the conquest of the Americas. His Black Legend provided Spain's imperial rivals in the New World, and Spain's critics—especially Protestant sectors—with the fuel needed to condemn that great Catholic kingdom.

However, Las Casas did not kick off the concerted defense of the Amerindians. That honor belonged to a Dominican friar, Father Antonio Montesino, in 1511. The violent subjugation of the Amerindians, coupled with ignoring the Christian obligation to bring the faith to pagans, was the subject of this most famous sermon in the history of the Americas. Unanimously approved by the Dominicans on Hispaniola, the sermon was preached by Montesino in Santo Domingo, 1511.[16] Montesino's sermon was a ringing denouncement of the oppression and insensitivity of the conquistadors and slaveholders (see Document 8). He demanded justice and mercy in the face of the injustice and inhumanity of the *encomiendas*. Las Casas may have heard the sermon since he was on the island in 1511, or, more likely, heard about it and got a transcript from Montesino himself. Las Casas later recorded the sermon in his *History of the Indies*.

Upon his return to Spain in 1515, Las Casas decided that the monarchs and their counselor had been deceived into thinking all was well in the settlement of the New World, and he made it his lifelong duty to set the record straight, employing history and law to his service. If good monarchs did not correct injustices and right wrongs, there was a price to pay: "Look, look to your souls, Your Lordships [members of the Council of the Indies that oversaw affairs in the Americas] and Mercies! For I greatly fear and greatly doubt of your salvation."

Las Casas then added, "Avoid like the plague—if you would be saved and would apply remedy to all of this misery—placing any credence in the counsel, letters, or spoken words of the ravening wolves here."[17]

Las Casas quickly grasped the gravity of the conquest, the ultimate consequence of it all. While the Amerindians lost their dignity, their land, their freedom, and, ultimately, their lives, the Spaniards were condemning themselves to eternal perdition. Hell, both in this life and the next, could be the only end for such impunity.

To liberate the Indians from the expanding tentacles of the *encomienda* system, and to save Spaniards from their iniquity, Las Casas passionately turned against the idea and practice of conquest in 1514 like the Dominicans of Hispaniola earlier. He took the pulpit on Pentecost Sunday and preached a sermon to his listeners in the small settlement of Espíritu Santo in Cuba that shocked them. Unless they gave up their *encomiendas*, unless they made full restitution for the wrongs done, unless they followed the narrow path of neighbor love, salvation was beyond their reach.

Las Casas the *encomendero* had become Las Casas the prophet, proclaiming the Word of God as he had come to understand it through the Dominicans of Hispaniola. His career from that Pentecost Sunday in 1514 to his death in 1566 was devoted to defending the Indians and attacking his antagonists with all the strength and knowledge and experience he could muster. The good friar proved to be one of the most formidable legal advocates of the sixteenth century, and perhaps in modern history.

What made Las Casas particularly effective was not only his eloquence and persistence but also his ability to penetrate to the very highest circles of Spanish power—to the Holy Roman Emperor Charles V and his son King Phillip II (both Spanish kings) themselves—and lay the unvarnished truth before them. Characteristically, for example, soon after Las Casas preached his sermon at Espíritu Santo he returned to Spain and took the issue straight to the aged King Ferdinand. Ferdinand died before ruling on Las Casas's petitions, but his young grandson Charles (who would succeed to the throne as Charles I of Spain and the Emperor Charles V) proved to be an apt listener to the impassioned priest over the next three decades.

In the meantime, Spain was developing as a great European and international power, outdoing even Portugal's imperial reach. Europe emerged from a long period of insularity following the collapse of the Roman Empire a thousand years earlier, and Spain became the leader of her rivals—England and France, for example—in moving beyond her old national borders on the Iberian Peninsula in this new era of European imperialism. Europe started to capture the world with her navies and armies and conquistadors, beginning with the Portuguese in Africa followed by the Spanish across the Atlantic, setting the example for other European peoples. Las Casas stood out in this era of growing imperialism, but as a critic. This role was precisely what made him (in)famous.

Las Casas in fact became the most notable—and some would say notorious—defender of Amerindians in his lifetime. His native advocacy emerged intellectually and spiritually out of a deeply held commitment to the liberty and equality of all humankind as he interpreted Scripture. He drew on the greatest of the Church thinkers and theologians—St. Augustine and St. Thomas Aquinas among them—upon canon or Church law, upon legal principles dating back to the Roman empire, and even sometimes to the great classical philosophers and historians of Greece and Rome to hammer out his defense: Amerindians could *only* be converted and brought to the faith by peaceful persuasion. Anything less was a travesty of the teachings of Jesus Christ.

In all the unjust violence waged in the name of preaching Christianity and civilizing native Americans, there is "not one jot of right," Las Casas reported pointedly. "For if it is truly by fears and terrors that those peoples be subjugated, then according to the natural and human and divine law all the rest that these men do is naught but air, save it be in atonement for those sins that shall cast them into the infernal fires, and likewise for the harm and offense they do the king and queen of Castile."[18] The friar was an outspoken critic of colonial injustice without relinquishing his intractable religious and political identity.

"All humankind is one," Las Casas later proclaimed, long before principles such as political equality fueled the intellectual passion of the eighteenth century that led to the American and French Revolutions (see Document 14). Las Casas possessed a remarkably "modern" political imagination that emphasized not only the inherent equality and natural freedom of all human beings but also the consent of the people and the limits of royal power as core principles of any legitimate government.

Just as Las Casas was preaching a very modern-style defense of American Indians based on the novel concept that "all humankind is one" or equal, at least in Christian principles, another friar, almost an exact contemporary of Las Casas, was leading a revolutionary movement that erupted in 1517. Martin Luther was born in 1483 and on October 31, 1517, he helped initiate the Protestant Reformation with his famous ninety-five theses posted on the church doors of Wittenberg, Germany, condemning the Roman Catholic Church for many errors in doctrine and practice. The battle was joined between Luther and his followers and the Church. With its center in Rome, the papacy rose to defend itself against the growing Reformation, which by 1530–1540 had bitterly divided the Church between Catholics and Protestant reformers.

The Spanish church remained the steadiest in defense of Roman Catholicism in the face of Protestant criticisms and defiance in this period, precisely when the conquest of the Americas was proceeding rapidly. Las Casas and Luther never met, nor does Las Casas mention the highly charged moments marking the advance of the Reformation across Europe, such as the meetings of the Council of Trent between 1545 and 1563 to determine the Church's responses to the Reformation. Las Casas's defense of Amerindians brought immensely persuasive and erudite evidence to the table, both from religious laws and natural moral law. But his battles were largely separate from the great issues dividing Christendom in Europe, such as the practice of selling indulgences and the doctrine of justification by grace. One relevant point of contrast between Las Casas and Luther concerned the matter of ecclesiastical power. Whereas Luther in Europe saw it as a ploy to protect corrupt clergy from civil authority, Las Casas saw it as a last line of defense against the Spanish abuses of Amerindians.

Let's recall that this was the sixteenth century, long before instant communications and information was at our fingertips twenty-four hours a day. Letters and communications took weeks between cities, and sometimes months between Europe and the Americas. Las Casas's work and that of his supporters in the recondite corners of Spain's new transatlantic empire, such as Guatemala, Venezuela, Mexico, and Peru, was far from the controversies in Europe set off by the Reformation, and so little of this increasingly bitter division in Christendom is reflected in Las Casas's writings.

But, in his own corner of concentration, he practiced what he preached. If Amerindians were indeed rational, civilized people, then they should be treated as equals, not subordinated by Spanish arrogance and military superiority. He not only waged his war in the intellectual, philosophical, and political circles of influence, but he also carried his battles to the New World itself, putting into practice his theories and eventually serving in the 1540s as Bishop of Chiapa in southern Mexico and northern Guatemala.

Las Casas viewed himself not simply as a messenger, prophet, and protector, but as an activist. What good were words without actions? What good was faith without works as the Epistle of James recorded in the New Testament? Over the years, Las Casas either sponsored directly or was heavily involved in several projects to change the nature of the conquest and colonization of the New World, and to alleviate the suffering of the Amerindians.

Remarkably, he could criticize imperial expansion without abandoning his loyalty to the Spanish Crown and Emperor Charles V. This paradoxical commitment to both protecting the natives and supporting Spain, or to defending native cultures and spreading Latin Christianity, makes him a challenging figure to understand today. For some, Las Casas represents a more benevolent face of empire in the Western scramble to control trade, seize land, and exploit natural resources outside Europe.[19] His noble sympathies for the plight of natives might seem ultimately vain, even insidious, because of his efforts to convert them to Christianity and incorporate them into the Spanish Crown. Regardless of his peaceful methods, Las Casas can look like a "militant Catholic imperialist" whose universal religious aspirations become indistinguishable from his Spanish imperial citizenship.[20] Overall, his religious commitments might seem to restrict a deeper humanitarianism, allowing fuller recognition of equality and greater respect for cultural difference.[21]

These are all possible ways of critically engaging Las Casas in our modern, indeed postmodern, times. But there is a more balanced approach to early modern Spain that locates the friar within a legal culture of competing rights and titles, thus allowing his prominent critical voice to rise above the sea of justifications for conquest.[22] From this standpoint, his religious ideas belong more clearly to the historical context of Renaissance and Reformation Europe, where faith challenged the status quo and even inspired social change through a greater appreciation of individual dignity and conscience. Las Casas's decision to become a Dominican friar and follow Montesino, then, was what enabled his prophetic voice on behalf of natives to condemn the violent political and economic forces of empire.

Las Casas's staunch opposition to imperial conquest and colonial practices should be viewed as an evolution over his reformist career, marked by both success and failure.[23] His failures were monumental, like his successes. He failed dismally in experiments on the island of Hispaniola in 1517 and 1518, and later, along the Venezuelan coast of the South American mainland in the early 1520s, to establish colonies of hard-working, honest Spanish yeomen devoted to a virtuous existence alongside natives.

One of his most dramatic mishaps occurred near Cumaná on the Venezuelan coast. Everything that could go wrong did so. Spanish slave raids had preceded him and poisoned the atmosphere of trust and faith that Las Casas hoped to establish among the Amerindians. The peasant farmers Las Casas had recruited in Spain took off as soon as they could, enticed by the quicker profits promised in the trading of captured native slaves deemed hostile. Some Dominican and Franciscan friars were martyred by angry Amerindians who lumped all Spaniards into the same category.

Adding proverbial insult to injury, when Las Casas returned to Hispaniola at the end of the fiasco, the ship set him ashore on the wrong end of the island.

Before reaching Santo Domingo, Las Casas and his little group were resting from the heat of the afternoon near Yaguana when some travelers from Santo Domingo met with them.

"So, what's new back in Castile or in Santo Domingo?" Las Casas's companions asked.

"Well, nothing much, although we heard the cleric Bartolomé de las Casas and all of his companions were killed by the Indians of the Pearl Coast."[24]

"That's impossible!" About that time Las Casas awoke with all the yelling and realized what was happening.

He was crushed. He felt bankrupted spiritually as the experiment was a profound failure.

The New Dominican

He entered a Dominican monastery in Hispaniola in 1522 and the next year was confirmed as a member of the Order of Preachers. Turning to the contemplative life for most of the 1520s, Las Casas read Scripture, prayed, and reflected on his life, his faith, theology, law, and the principles of Christianity measured against the conquest and colonization of the New World. In 1527, his superiors sent him to the northern coastal town of Puerto de Plata to found a Dominican house. There he built a small stone monastery, planted a garden, and, in the quiet and fertile peace of the small port, also began to compile and write his *History of the Indies*, a work that eventually reached monumental proportions and occupied him for the rest of his life. Telling history became the principal vehicle for advocating on behalf of Amerindians and their freedom. Like the first Dominicans of Hispaniola, Las Casas began "to combine the idea of right with reality."[25] In other words, the struggle for justice demanded first and foremost a recognition of rights that were denied to Amerindian peoples. His *History* became one of the first and most famous of the chronicles of the rise of Spain's empire in the Indies and its moral consequences.

The three-volume *History* is one of the most detailed resources for the early presence of Spain in the Indies, beginning with Christopher Columbus's first voyage and reaching to about 1520 in chronology. It also recorded the earlier Portuguese conquest of Africa. Las Casas was not simply a chronicler; he was commentator, interpreter, polemicist, and advocate, even while he putatively attempted to remain true to the muse of history. He wanted, in fact, to "set the record straight," which is why many historians with a particular perspective or ideology write history (see document 7). In his *History*, he included the diary/log of Christopher Columbus's signal first voyage of 1492–1493. The original of that log was lost, but not before Las Casas abstracted most of it and wove it into his first volume of the *History*. He thus preserved the record of the greatest voyage in Western civilization given its impact on the rise of empires and, in the long run, global history.

Perhaps the greatest drawback to a chronicler writing about his own times is also paradoxically the greatest strength: his closeness to the subject and events, or, as in the case of Las Casas, an eyewitness to much of what he recorded. That produces a powerful narrative imbued with a ring of authenticity that no secondary account can match. On the other hand, being so close to the events also clouds the issue with a myopic nearness that cannot be addressed except through the passage of time. A chronicler lacks the benefit of perspective, a separation of time, and perhaps even space from the events one is writing about. As Las Casas began to compose his massive historical treatise in the relative quiet of Puerto Plata, the conquest swept across Mexico and Peru, soon to be Spain's richest New World colonies boasting of gold and silver mines.

Although rather isolated physically in Puerto Plata, Las Casas did not lose touch with events in the Empire. His letters and memorials condemning Indian slavery and the *encomienda* were presented at the Spanish court by his friends with regularity. In 1530, for example, an antislavery decree suggested by Las Casas or one of his allies was issued by the Emperor Charles V. But opposition to Las Casas was growing also, from church officials and *encomenderos* alike.

Defenders of the conquistadors claimed the mainland Indians were but beastly practitioners of human sacrifice on an enormous scale. They were allegedly incapable of ever becoming Christians through peaceful means. Some were cannibals, testifying to their brutish nature. And did not the greatest authority of natural law, Aristotle—an ancient Greek philosopher of notable repute—divide men into those born to serve and those born to govern on the basis of presence or absence of rationality?[26] (See Document 11.) Like Moors, these native barbarians should be forced to accept Christian culture and its laws, even though their conversion and ultimate allegiances were always suspect.

Las Casas crafted a powerful response in defense of the Indians, with peace outlining the only way to seek their conversion (see Document 12). The Indians *were* capable of understanding the faith and not doomed to extinction for their past sins as some Spanish friars and theologians claimed. Just the opposite was true, he wrote. The Lord God commanded believers to preach to *all* peoples. "Therefore, it followed that all peoples had the capacity," for "the 'elect' chosen for salvation were among all peoples—and that included the Indians."[27]

Not unlike some of the nomadic Old Testament prophets or apostles of the early Church, Las Casas became a peripatetic missionary over the next several decades. He embarked for Peru late in 1534, bent on joining a small contingent of Dominican friars to spread the faith in the land of the Inca. But they never reached their destination. A combination of contrary winds and currents, and maddening doldrums, drove them back to Panama, and from there they took passage to Nicaragua, more conveniently reached by favoring winds.

While in Nicaragua in 1536, he berated the conquistadors for enslaving and brutalizing the Amerindians with relative impunity in this colony so remote from royal control.[28] Thousands of Nicaraguan Indians had been enslaved and shipped off to Panama and Peru. In an atmosphere where "[Spanish] settlers flogged the natives for wasting time to learn about Christianity from Las Casas and his friars," Las Casas's choleric temperament kicked in. He preached such powerful sermons that, on one occasion, incensed by the wild friar's attacks, he was "pulled down from the pulpit by order of the governor's wife."[29] It was obvious to Las Casas that these people meant business. He could do little in such a place, so he headed with his fellow friars for Mexico and Guatemala to the west and north.

In Guatemala, he was given the opportunity to put his first book, *The Only Way*, into practice. Short for *The Only Way of Attracting All Peoples to the True Religion*, this treatise argued passionately for the peaceful evangelization of Amerindians with extensive citations from Scripture, early Christian writings, canon law, and philosophy. The unprecedented treatise condemned the Spanish missionary wars of conquest as patently unjust and tyrannical (see Document 21).

Bishop of Chiapa

In 1540 Las Casas returned to Spain after a twenty-year absence. This trip led to one of the high points of Las Casas's career, the issuing of a set of New Laws for the Indies in 1542 incorporating most of Las Casas's suggestions for reform.[30] It was preceded by a crucial bull issued on June 9, 1537, by Pope Paul III (see Document 15). Bulls were official letters written by popes that contained essential declarations or teachings meant for Catholic Christians. *Sublimis Deus*, inspired by Las Casas's *The Only Way*, proclaimed the inherent rationality of the Amerindians and their freedom to accept Christianity without the diabolical threat of violence. They were not "beasts who talked," as some conquistadors loudly proclaimed.

Back in Spain, Las Casas turned to direct action once again. He worked feverishly through 1541 and most of 1542 to change the laws that governed the Indies. "Las Casas's technique in achieving these goals was powerful and dramatic. For hours without interruption he held the councilors motionless with a complete reading of the *Decimation* (the memorial on atrocities), while his two aides, the friar and the Indian, displayed piles of notarized proofs to back what he was describing. No less powerful was his impassioned presentation of *Twenty Reasons Against the Encomienda*—and the first reason was that the papal Bull of Donation [1493] could only be a grant for conversion."[31] That kind of conversion insisted upon the freedom of Amerindians to accept or refuse Christianity (see Document 10).

The New Laws of the Indies were promulgated November 20, 1542 (see Document 9). They constituted a sweeping set of reforms that attacked the *encomienda* system, abolished Amerindian slavery, and prohibited future wars of conquest. The decrees shocked the conquistador-*encomendero* class across the Americas.[32] In retrospect, they point to a marked contrast between the legal regime of the Spanish New World and the antebellum South on the status of dispossessed laborers.[33]

Spanish opponents clearly felt the crazed cleric was once more on the assault, and they were squarely in the crosshairs of his sights. As a reward for his services, the Emperor offered Las Casas the bishopric of Chiapa.[34] He was consecrated bishop in Seville on March 30, 1544, and sailed for the Indies that summer. Traveling with Las Casas were more than forty Dominicans from Spain, many from Salamanca, recruited by the new bishop for missionary work. The fleet arrived in Santo Domingo on September 9, 1544.

Las Casas was received, along with his retinue, as a pariah in the Indies.

"The processional march of his devout young friars, following the example of Sevillan religious brotherhoods, was greeted not with sympathy but with jeers and ridicule. The populace refused to offer hospitality or food . . . or even to hear their sermons during the three months they had to wait for further passage."[35] Rebuffed in Santo Domingo, Las Casas soon suffered even more attacks as he traveled to his bishopric of Chiapa, his place of overseeing the local flock of believers, in southern New Spain.

Across Spanish America, the New Laws provoked not only resentment but also outright rebellion on the part of the settlers. In Peru, the first viceroy sent by the crown to govern the new colony—Blasco Núñez Vela—was captured and beheaded by Gonzalo Pizarro, who was leading a rebel faction determined to keep Peru for itself rather than acquiesce to royal control from Spain. Royal officials in other parts of the Indies refused to enforce most of the New Laws, especially the more onerous ones, such as outlawing Indian slavery and disinheriting the *encomenderos*.

Upon arriving in Ciudad Real, the capital of his see in Chiapa, the new bishop flung down the gauntlet at his slaveholding parishioners. Like the Dominicans of Hispaniola decades before, Las Casas, now a bishop, exercised his episcopal power to coerce Spanish *encomenderos* to observe the New Laws. Everyone guilty of extortionate and inhumane practices toward Amerindians in the *encomienda* had to repent, confess, and make amends. Otherwise, no confession would be heard, no absolution or forgiveness of sins offered, and, ultimately, excommunication would follow. To be excommunicated meant separation from the Church and, in Roman Catholic doctrine, it was an obstacle to an individual's salvation. Excommunication for believers was like a sentence of eternal death and suffering.

Bishop Las Casas advanced a pro-Indian policy through his "Rules for Confessors" (or *Confesionario*).[36] He made it a prerogative of penitent *encomenderos*, conquerors, and arms-dealer priests to draw up a public document in accordance with conscience and the advice of the confessor that stipulated the manner of restitution toward Amerindians.[37] The public document was then enforceable under the local bishop through Church courts. Additionally, the "Rules for Confessors" declared all Spanish wars of conquest in the Indies unjust. Such a bold claim challenging the entire Spanish colonial project was tantamount to high treason.[38]

The settlers flung back the challenge in Las Casas's face, with swords drawn, at the controversial Bishop who threatened their very livelihood in this life, and their souls in the next. One cleric, Dean Gil Quintana, "openly disobeyed him and, sword in hand . . . resisted the bishop's officials and fled to Gracias a Dios [Honduras], where he turned the recently installed Audiencia de los Confines against Las Casas."[39] The *audiencias* were legislative-judicial bodies of government operating alongside viceroys, governors, and others by directly representing the king's interests.

Not only were swords drawn, but words also flew, filled with indignation, plain and simple insults that could have worn down a sturdier spirit than the Bishop of Chiapa. The townspeople rose in a near riot, demanding retractions from the bishop, clamoring before him, waving Pope Alexander VI's 1493 Bull of Donation (*Inter caetera*) to justify war and enslavement, buzzing loudly that this bishop, "a disturber of the peace . . . a foe of Christians and a protector of Indian dogs," must go.[40]

The name-calling escalated. Street urchins passing below the bishop's residence parroted scurrilous songs; others slung insults ranging from "fool!" to "glutton!"; and some questioned his lineage and his religion. One idiot, moved by the increasingly strident cacophony, fired off a harquebus outside Las Casas's window, probably pleased with himself and congratulated by his cronies for striking terror into the bishop's heart.

For the next two years, until the middle of 1547 when Las Casas returned to Spain, he sparred with his enemies in Guatemala and Mexico. He threatened to excommunicate the Viceroy and all the judges of the *Audiencia* of New Spain. In short, he went about his business with characteristic disdain for his personal safety and totally committed to relieving the afflictions of the Indians.

At mid-century, the Emperor Charles V, prompted by Las Casas and his allies, called one of the most remarkable councils in Western political history to answer the questions: Were the conquests truly unjust, as Las Casas claimed? Or were they entirely moral and necessary for spreading the faith, as Juan Ginés de Sepúlveda (1490–1573), one of Spain's great humanist scholars, claimed, based on his interpretation of Aristotle's taxonomy of humankind? Las Casas insisted that the conquests be halted and all Indians turned over directly to the Crown as originally intended by the New Laws of 1542.[41]

The Great Debate of 1550

Las Casas persuaded the Emperor that his conscience, and perhaps his very salvation, was in jeopardy by the continuation of the conquests. Charles V instructed the Council of the Indies to convene a committee of theologians and jurists at Valladolid to discuss how transatlantic expansion may be conducted justly and with assurance of conscience. Charles suspended all conquests (April 16, 1550) until the new committee heard the debate and rendered a decision. Would that it had been that simple, or short, a process.

The principal question up for debate was whether the Indians of the

New World should be brought under Spanish rule through force—the nature of political conquest—to convert them to the Christian faith and civilize them with European customs and law. Sepúlveda was on the affirmative side defending the conquests. His *Democrates secundus* (1546) had already presented his arguments in detail. Sepúlveda began with a spirited three-hour defense in mid-August 1550. Las Casas, fully opposed to the conquests, as evidenced by his "Rules for Confessors," responded with a numbing five-day reading of his 500-page—give or take a few pages—tract entitled "The Defense . . . Against the Persecutors and Slanderers of the Peoples of the New World Discovered Across the Seas."[42] He read the entire tract in what the historian Lewis Hanke described as a "verbal onslaught."[43]

The judges retired to consider the issues. Overwhelmed by Las Casas's long arguments, they asked one of their members, the Dominican theologian and friend of Las Casas Domingo de Soto, to prepare a summary of the case.[44] Soto did so, adding Sepúlveda's reply to twelve major objections Las Casas had raised in his original presentation.

The next session did not occur until April and May 1551, when the judges reconvened in the Spanish city of Valladolid. In the meantime, Sepúlveda discovered, "much to his disgust, that Las Casas had availed himself of the interim period to prepare a rebuttal to Sepúlveda's replies."[45] We do not really know the final decision of the judges. Six or seven years later the Council of the Indies was still trying to collect opinions, and both Las Casas and Sepúlveda claimed victory.[46] Las Casas tells us that Sepúlveda tried submitting his earlier work *Democrates secundus* for publication under the Royal Council of Spain and for consideration at the Council of Trent. Both official bodies of church and state refused to endorse its "deadly poison."[47]

Las Casas, similar to Dominican theologians from the University of Salamanca such as Soto and Francisco de Vitoria, applied the view of natural law inspired by St. Thomas Aquinas to support the legitimacy and rights of Indian polities.[48] These Dominicans advocated that no civilizations—such as the Amerindian ones—lacked natural reason in their political affairs. They must not be targets of conquest and enslavement. Aristotle, along with Sepúlveda, had left conquest wide open by declaring that some peoples could be considered "natural slaves" for their alleged barbarism and irrational behavior. Las Casas opposed it vehemently; since all persons are made in the image of God, they are collectively equal and free (see Document 16). Moreover, as he concluded his Valladolid defense, he seized the moment to proclaim, "The Indians are our brothers, and Christ has given his life for them."

Las Casas's theological sympathies for the writings of Aquinas were integrated with his profound legal reasoning, which together provided him with the basic tools for defending the economic, political, and spiritual freedom of the Indians. He argued for Amerindian freedom from slavery, conquest, and forced conversion to the Christian faith. His prophetic side extended Aquinas's view of the natural law to account for natural subjective rights—or powers ascribed to individual persons immune from unlawful coercion—beginning with the rights of freedom, property, and self-governance irrespective of religious beliefs (see document 19).[49]

The Spanish theologians inspired by the thought of Aquinas argued that people should be free to enter into organized communities. Peoples enjoy a right of consenting to their respective leaders who are freely chosen. Las Casas could see in the great Indian "kingdoms" of the New World rational expressions of civilization (albeit not Christian) rather than barbarism. They entered communities, they "elected" leaders, and they formed human laws. Therefore, the Spanish kings have no authority to rule over them unless the entire community, indeed every person, freely consents (see Document 23).

In contrast, Sepúlveda argued that the Indians were unrefined, irrational, and idolatrous creatures prone to practice human sacrifice and cannibalism. Because they were supposedly entrenched in these immoral customs, they needed a superior civilization and religion—Catholic Spain—to discipline and educate them for their own good. Centuries later, the modern philosopher of liberalism John Stuart Mill would still be rehearsing a similar argument to justify British colonialism over the "backward" peoples of India. As Sepúlveda and his Spanish colonialist allies saw it, the papal Bull of Donation gave religious authorization for the Crown to evangelize and civilize by means of conquest. This Bull had basically divided the unknown world then just being explored and discovered by mariners such as Columbus into two spheres of Iberian influence between Portugal and Spain. It had also entrusted Spain with the duty "to instruct the natives . . . and to imbue them with the same Christian faith and sound morals."[50]

Sepúlveda was formed in a warrior brand of Renaissance humanism in Italy not unlike the better-known political thinker Niccolò Machiavelli. The Spaniard applied "humanist criteria" to rank foreign cultures on a scale descending from the European ideal.[51] When Sepúlveda surveyed the landscape of Amerindian polities, as told by Spanish chroniclers, his ultimate benchmark for labeling the native peoples irrational rested on the sensational practice of idolatry evident in human sacrifice. Nothing could be more contrary to natural law than the act of destroying innocent life. "By this cause alone," Sepúlveda confidently asserted before the council at Valladolid, the Indians "can be conquered and punished."[52]

The violation of natural law meant something radically different for Las Casas when seen from the perspective of oppressed Indians. Where Sepúlveda saw brute *irrationality* among natives, Las Casas saw the violation of Amerindian *rights*. Under Las Casas's erudition and advocacy, natural law was not a tool of imperial conquest, but an ethic of resistance to colonial power. Here lay the heart of the controversy that Las Casas opened in his "Rules for Confessors" and his *Defense of the Indians* at Valladolid: all the Spanish wars were unjust, and the Indians had the full right to defend themselves against an aggressor culture claiming superiority (see Document 17).

The bishop of Chiapa claimed, most daringly, that the Indians could wage a just war in defense of their false gods against any nation threatening to destroy them.[53] Las Casas went on to bury Sepúlveda under the weight of testimony drawn from his long experience in the Indies, and his extraordinary capacity to drink from a well-spring of tradition, history, philosophy, theology, and canon law. This confluence of ideas tested in the struggle for justice "is clearly a moment of first importance in the development of human rights."[54]

The issues debated at Valladolid in 1550–1551 belong to the history of religion and politics in the West. The political claims of the Spanish Crown over the Indies were called into question on essentially spiritual and moral grounds. If the wars against Amerindians were unjust, then the claims to sovereignty were mere usurpations. There could be *no* just title to the Indies, notwithstanding the papal bull of 1493, which Las Casas understood as Spain's privilege to preach on the strict condition that the Indians, every last one of them, must have their freedom and rights respected.

Las Casas and his like-minded allies had to tread lightly, however. Espousing the cause of the Indians sat well on the conscience of Charles V. Calling the claims of his grandfather and grandmother (Ferdinand and Isabel) to the Indies false and illegal patently made his own claims to sovereignty, jurisdiction, and authority weak and theoretically untenable. Notably, Las Casas never denied the Spanish right, by papal authority, to bring Christianity to the Americas. What he rejected outright was the coercive manner of its delivery. Again, this tension in his commitments has made him difficult to interpret in modern times.

Yet the conquest was painful reality. There was no going back. For Las Casas, the battle for the defense of the Indians had merely paused at midcentury. Still immensely vigorous, he now concentrated on the centers of power in Spain, where he waged his campaigns until his death in 1566 at the age of eighty-two.

The Everlasting Advocate

After getting his affairs in order so that he could later retire to live and work at the Dominican college of San Gregorio in Valladolid, Las Casas took off for Seville in 1552.[55] In Seville, the publishing capital of Spain, he wrote and published a number of important treatises. He took quarters in the Dominican monastery of San Pablo where the library of the late Hernando Columbus (Columbus's illegitimate second son) was located and continued composing and rewriting his massive *History of the Indies*. He also had access to the Columbus family archives in a chapel of the local Carthusian monastery.[56]

Hernando had not only written a biography of his father that Las Casas consulted, but Las Casas also found the abridged version of Columbus's original log of the first journey at San Carlos. Little did he know that he would be one of the last to see this historic document and perhaps the last to copy it, which he did and included it in his *History*. It is the only record of this precious log we have, since the original and several early copies disappeared.[57]

As he was working on his *History*, Las Casas also reworked several other treatises, including one that would ensure his fame, or infamy, for the next half millennium. His *An Account, Much Abbreviated, of the Destruction of the Indies* related the destruction of the Amerindians by the Spaniards (see Document 5).[58] Translated from its original Spanish into other languages and coupled with horrendous images, the *Destruction of the Indies* became the cornerstone of the Black Legend targeting the Spanish New World and the Holy Roman Empire. English and Dutch publicists, propagandists, and Protestants in general impaled Spaniards and Catholics (almost synonymous in the superheated religious debates that escalated into religious warfare in the sixteenth century) for extreme cruelty and barbarity in the treatment of Amerindians.[59]

Las Casas and the African Slave Trade

While in Seville—a port bustling with ships, sailors, masters, navigators, travelers, and African slaves employed on the docks and in the shops of this great maritime city—Las Casas pondered on the African slave trade. What had started out as an inconsequential suggestion by him more than thirty years earlier to reduce the suffering of the Amerindians by importing African slaves to take the place of Amerindians had turned into a growing, and sordid, trade in human flesh.

African slaves were introduced by Portuguese mariners into the Caribbean islands in the second decade of the sixteenth century to replenish the dwindling numbers of Amerindians and supply the labor-intensive metal mining that took hold on the islands, paving the path toward the modern sugar plantations. For a long time Las Casas was held accountable, in part at least, for having introduced African slavery in the New World in his effort to relieve the suffering of the Amerindians.

As he pored over the logs and narratives of Spanish and Portuguese merchants and navigators, such as Christopher Columbus himself, to Guinea and the Canary Islands, he began to perceive the nature of African slavery in its true deformed manner.[60] He denounced it in his *History* with a passion as he composed in the monastery of San Pablo (see Document 7).

The injustice of the African slave trade prompted him to not only re-evaluate (and deeply regret) his previous political judgment, but also his thinking about the just war tradition in the West. Although Las Casas faithfully proclaimed peaceful evangelization, he was not a pacifist opposed to all war. However, he approached war not abstractly but from concrete cases of injustice demanding reparation. Historical testimony provided him the means of doing so. The Portuguese conquest of Africa presented clear circumstances for judging when war was legitimate, especially against aggressors and violent persecutors. His imagination was held captive by the recorded cries of injured victims of Christian colonial expansion and conquest, beginning with the innocent peoples of Africa (see Document 22). According to natural law and human reason, both Christians and non-Christians could legitimately defend their sovereignty and religious customs from unjustified aggression.

The Inquisition Takes on Las Casas

In his long career denouncing injustices and the wrongs of the Conquest—and by extension, of the conquistador class itself—Las Casas may have been denounced to the Inquisition for heresy. What got him into trouble was his contention that the king had no authority to dispose of Amerindians, their life, their liberty, or their property through such institutions as the *encomienda*.[61] Las Casas's old nemesis, Sepúlveda, may have been behind the charges, but we cannot be certain.[62] The charge by the Inquisition attempted to stand on Scripture, drawing on the apostles Peter and Paul who, in various texts, ordered Christians to obey the authority of lords and kings. To question their wisdom and their acts constituted not only *lèse majesté*, but also treason, which was equated easily with heresy in the Spain of the sixteenth century.[63] They were in fact interchangeable. If one were convicted of heresy, it was not only a crime against the Church, but also against the Christian ruler of land—the king or emperor. Nothing came of the Inquisition's threat, while the offending tract written by Las Casas, *De regia potestate* (*On Royal Power*), which contained some truly astonishing assertions about political life, was eventually published posthumously in 1571 in Germany.

What *did* Las Casas contend later in life that so got under the skin of his detractors? Read one way, *De regia potestate* was nothing less than a ringing political precursor of the modern concept of rule by free consent of the people, though one grounded ultimately in divine sovereignty instead of the general will of the people (see Document 18). Taking his cues from the Bible, Las Casas noted in one of his other late works that the Israelite kings Saul and David illustrated two necessary principles underlying every genuine and legitimate form of political authority: divine providence and the free election by the people.[64] Divine providence signifies the wisdom of God that orders everything in the world in ways often inconceivable to human beings.

Las Casas believed that the governing authority must be a minister of the law, not its inventor. "The whole basis of Casas' argument," wrote Wagner and Parish, "is that kings, although sovereign, have no illimitable power; they are servants of nations, and the people make kings, who must rule for their good. From this general doctrine, Casas goes on to attack the grants of fief, denying the royal right to alienate territory or give certain fiefs without the consent of the feudatory. Therefore—this was obviously what he was driving at—*encomiendas* were tyrannical and the King must order restitution of unjustly acquired Spanish property in the Indies."[65]

Las Casas took the argument further. "This was a virtual denial of the King's authority to grant *encomiendas*, and Casas rested it on a sweeping *doctrine of popular rights* [emphasis added]. Under the 'natural rights of man,' he asserted, all men and their affairs are free and to be ruled only for their own benefit; royal ordinances are null when contrary to the interests of the people."[66] This really was a subversive doctrine, attributing legitimate authority to the will of the people under God, rather than granting absolute power to kings appointed by God. And, if one moves a little further in the historical record, we find the roots of that subversive and revolutionary experiment in government, invoking this very same principle, to justify the American Revolution.

Las Casas and the Legacy of Human Rights

The remarkable legacy of Las Casas as a faith-filled advocate for the rights of dispossessed peoples and promoter of political independence has remained strong over the centuries, especially in Latin America. Historian Edward Cleary once noted that "since Las Casas's death, a continuous discourse has taken place in Latin America about dignity, rights, and freedom."[67] Las Casas's name has been associated with revolutionary leaders of social and political movements in Latin America from Simón Bolívar to José Martí. The legacy of the friar's defense of native resistance to colonial powers ran deep in Latin American political history.

Bolívar, the greatest of the Liberators during the Latin American Wars of Independence in the early nineteenth century, once referred to Las Casas as "the apostle of the Americas" and dreamed of naming the capital of his pan-American union of republics after the bishop of Chiapa. The Cuban poet and social revolutionary Martí was the principal actor in the long struggle for Cuban independence from Spain in the second half of the nineteenth century. Martí wrote an essay "El Padre Las Casas" in his effort to mobilize the Cuban independence movement. The essay reflected on the justice and compassion of the bishop, who "went to Chiapa to weep with the Indians." Highlighting the friar's political legacy, Martí wrote that Las Casas heroically defended "the human right to liberty, and the duty of rulers to respect it."[68]

Las Casas was also one of the principal inspirations for the twentieth-century movement in Latin America known as liberation theology. According to the pioneer of liberation theology, Dominican priest Gustavo Gutiérrez, Las Casas provided a crucial methodological starting point in that movement's preferential option for the poor, which arises from the perspective of the victims of poverty and oppression. Gutiérrez explained the friar's legacy as "a declaration of the rights of the poor," which is what ultimately "bestows on human rights in general an authentic universality."[69]

The universality of the Gospel message for Las Casas meant that every person intended to hear it must have the freedom to receive it on his or her own terms and never by force. This radical commitment to spiritual freedom was an idea sweeping across Western Europe in the sixteenth century. Las Casas articulated a robust doctrine of equality, freedom, and rights for all persons and peoples, irrespective of religion or race. Today, there are centers and institutes of human rights across Mexico and Peru in his name dedicated to the ongoing struggle for justice among indigenous and marginalized peoples. His ethic of resisting unjust profit-seeking retains appeal in addressing new forms of colonialism in Latin America like land appropriation and water privatization strengthened by international trade and multinational corporations.

Similar to war, Las Casas never spoke of rights in the abstract, but always referred to the reality of the poor and oppressed Amerindians. Furthermore, he believed that the ultimate authority of rights was not political or pragmatic, but rather spiritual and metaphysical, because it flowed from divine sovereignty and natural law. The community in the world entrusted with the task of protecting the rights of all innocent peoples was the Church, or the community of the faithful, with bishops as shepherds and the pope its visible head. (See Document 25.)

Las Casas's zealous advocacy for Indians in his role of bishop of Chiapa can make him look obsessed with clerical power. However, as someone trained in the canon law of the Church, he knew that he could appeal to his episcopal power only when secular courts failed to enforce the New Laws. Bishop Las Casas followed the strategy of Montesino and the Dominicans of Hispaniola by disciplining slaveholders in the confessional. The uncompromising message of the first Dominicans was, after all, what inspired Las Casas to reverse his position on slaveholding and turn toward pro-Indian advocacy.

If all people were created in God's image as the Bible so clearly states, then all humanity was the same across the diverse spectrum of human laws, cultures, and traditions. Las Casas simplified it: Amerindians in the New World had equal rights as Spaniards in all things pertaining to natural law and the law of nations, regardless of their religious differences. Indeed, he spoke about an inherent right of both Amerindians and Africans to defend themselves from foreign Iberian aggressors, and to govern themselves freely. But Las Casas went even further. The Incas of Peru, he argued, had a right to their sacred possessions as well as their sacred kingships, which, in turn, demanded that the Spaniards repair injustices inflicted on them and restore their rights. At their core, the Indians possess an inborn human desire to serve a superior power or supreme being—God—just as Christians do (see Document 20).

Las Casas's profound respect for the religious and cultural lives of non-Christians in the New World relied on a canon legal principle of toleration from the Middle Ages. Strikingly, Las Casas mined what was best in medieval thinking on Christian relations with Jews and Muslims to carve out the spiritual immunity of Indians from the judgments of Christians (see Document 24).

As a true innovator, Las Casas applied the traditional legal norm of toleration to the New World context. The implications were outstanding from a political standpoint: he ruled out immorality and idolatry—the standard justifications used by Spaniards against the Indians—as legitimate grounds for war. Not unlike Protestant reformers in the Old World, Las Casas promoted religious rights for persons in error. These rights applied not only to individuals, but also to entire communities and peoples outside of Christianity.[70] At the end of his life, Las Casas wrote a letter to Pope Pius V requesting one last time that the papacy take the side of oppressed and impoverished Amerindian peoples by excommunicating anyone who wished to wage an unjust war against them by forcing them to be Christian (see Document 26).

Conclusion

In 1561, Las Casas moved to the Dominican monastery at Atocha in Madrid. He remained active, corresponding with fellow clerics, largely Dominicans, across the Americas, arguing his causes with energy and conviction. They sought his advice and counsel, and he responded with vigor, this oldest defender of Amerindians.

He passed away on July 18, 1566, and was buried two days later.[71] Busy until the end, Las Casas not only wrote a letter to Pope Pius V, calling upon him to take up the challenge of rectifying the errors of the Conquest. Just a few days before his death, he also presented a long memorial to the Council of the Indies, describing and defending his positions, advocating radical reforms—restitution of all Indian properties, restoration of Indian sovereignty, etc.—that would never come to pass.

Las Casas had, in fact, outlived the reform spirit of his earlier years, although his soul and his pen never quieted in favor of the Indians. The Spanish occupation of the Indies was a fact. Future expeditions—into Florida, into northern Mexico, into New Mexico, and into other frontiers of the Empire as it was now taking shape—carried disclaimers and clauses protecting the Indians, but they were honored more in the breach than in fact. That there was a breach recognized at all suggested the seed of conscience had been planted by Montesino, Las Casas, and many others.

Over his long life, Las Casas therefore did achieve an extraordinary goal: lifting the Amerindian before the Spanish, and European, conscience. Long before modern practitioners began to seek out the "other" voices in history—people who left few written or documentary records to remember them by—Las Casas discovered and advocated on behalf of their voices in the Conquest of the Indies. He did so with passion and conviction, directing his voice to the heights of kings and emperors, seeking redress for the wrongs and sins committed by several generations of his countrymen.

In doing so, he pioneered a new understanding of universal rights. He was prompted by the extraordinary discovery of a new world and a new people that challenged Europeans to accommodate to a part of the universe they knew nothing of before Columbus returned to Spain in the winter of 1492–1493. The complexity and scope of Las Casas the historian, the missionary, the advocate, the political philosopher, and the canon lawyer is difficult to summarize in these pages. However, his singular commitment to proclaiming the truth that all humankind is one family endowed with basic rights provides a unique vantage point for once again returning to this dynamic figure in our pluralistic global society where justice and freedom can never be taken for granted.

As you read the documents of the era in the following pages, feel the fires of passion and conviction that light the subject in a way no secondary account can. And no other author of the sixteenth century felt and wrote with such gravity and faith as Bartolomé de las Casas.

THE DOCUMENTS

I

The "New" World

All stories have a beginning, and the first voyage of Christopher Columbus inaugurated the exploration and settlement of the New World that transformed global history. The first document describes, through the eyes of Columbus and Las Casas, the moment in time when Columbus made landfall on October 12, 1492, after a long voyage into the unknown reaches of the Atlantic Ocean. Along with the second document, which describes Columbus's arrival at the Court of Isabel and Ferdinand in Barcelona in the spring of 1493, one can easily sense the thrill of the Spanish reaction to the Columbian discovery.

Document 1. "At two hours after midnight the land appeared": Christopher Columbus's First Voyage to America, 1492–1493

The following is Las Casas's transcription of the diary (or log) of Columbus's first voyage to the Americas, 1492.[1] This excerpt records the end of the voyage, the excitement of discovering land after many weeks at sea, and the landing of Columbus and some of his men on the island of San Salvador (Watlings Island). What are Columbus's impressions of the native people? How do these impressions or descriptions fit into Spain's colonial project?

Wednesday, 10 October

He steered west-southwest; they traveled ten miles per hour and at times 12 and for a time seven and between day and night made 59 leagues; he told the men only 44 leagues. Here the men could no longer stand it; they complained of the long voyage. But the Admiral encouraged them as best he could, giving them good hope of the benefits that they would be able to secure. And he added that it was useless to complain since he had come to find the Indies and thus had to continue the voyage until he found them, with the help of Our Lord.

Thursday, 11 October

He steered west-southwest. They took much water aboard, more than they had taken in the whole [entire] voyage. They saw petrels and a green bulrush near the ship. The men of the caravel *Pinta* saw a cane and a stick, and took on board another small stick that appeared to have been worked with iron, and a piece of cane and other vegetation originating on land, and a small plank. The men of the caravel *Niña* also saw other signs of land and a small stick loaded [covered with] with barnacles. With these signs everyone breathed more easily and cheered up. On this day, up to sunset, they made [covered] 27 leagues.

After sunset he steered on his former course to the west. They made about 12 miles each hour and, until two hours after midnight, made about 90 miles, which is twenty-two leagues and a half. And because the caravel *Pinta* was a better sailor and went ahead of the Admiral it found land and made the signals that the Admiral had ordered. A sailor named Rodrigo de Triana saw this land first, although the Admiral, at the tenth hour of the night, while he was on the sterncastle, saw a light, although it was something so faint that he did not wish to affirm that it was land. But he called Pero Gutiérrez, the steward of the king's dais, and told him that there seemed to be a light, and for him to look; and thus he did and saw it. He also told Rodrigo Sánchez de Segovia, whom the king and queen were sending as *veedor* [comptroller] of the fleet, who saw nothing because he was not in a place where he could see it. After the Admiral said it, it was seen once or twice; and it was like a small wax candle that rose and lifted, which to a few seemed to be an indication of land. But the Admiral was certain that they were near land, because of which when they recited the *Salve*, which sailors in their own way are accustomed to recite and sing, all being present, the Admiral entreated and admonished them to keep a good lookout on the forecastle and to watch carefully for land; At two hours after midnight the land appeared, from which they were about two leagues distant. They hauled down all the sails and kept only the *treo*, which is the mainsail without bonnets, and jogged on

and off, passing time until daylight Friday, when they reached an
islet of the Lucayas, which was called Guanahani in the language
of the Indians. Soon they saw naked people; and the Admiral went
ashore in the armed launch, and Martín Alonso Pinzón and his
brother Vicente Anes, who was captain of the *Niña*. The Admiral brought out the royal banner and the captains two flags with the
green cross, which the Admiral carried on all the ships as a standard, with an F and a Y, and over each letter a crown, one on one
side of the cross and the other on the other side. Thus put ashore
they saw very green trees and many ponds and fruits of various
kinds. The Admiral called to the two captains and to the others
who had jumped ashore and to Rodrigo Descobedo, the *escrivano*
[secretary or ship's clerk] of the whole fleet, and to Rodrigo Sánchez
de Segovia; and he said that they should be witnesses that, in the
presence of all, he would take, as in fact he did take, possession of
the said island for the king and for the queen his lords, making the
declarations that were required, and which at more length are contained in the testimonials made there in writing. Soon many people
of the island gathered there. What follows are the very words of
the Admiral in his book about his first voyage to, and discovery of,
these Indies. I, he says, in order that they would be friendly to us—
because I recognized that they were people who would be better
freed (from error) and converted to our Holy Faith by love than by
force—to some of them I gave red caps, and glass beads which they
put on their chests, and many other things of small value, in which
they took so much pleasure and became so much our friends that
it was a marvel. Later they came swimming to the ships' launches
where we were and brought us parrots and cotton thread in balls
and javelins and many other things, and they traded them to us for
other things which we gave them, such as small glass beads and
bells. In sum, they took everything and gave of what they had very
willingly. But it seemed to me that they were a people very poor in
everything. All of them go around as naked as their mothers bore
them; and the women also, although I did not see more than one
quite young girl. And all those I saw were young people, for none
did I see of more than 30 years of age. They are very well formed,
with handsome bodies and good faces. Their hair [is] coarse—
almost like the tail of a horse—and short. They wear their hair
down over their eyebrows except for a little in the back which they
wear long and never cut. Some of them paint themselves with black,
and they are of the color of the Canarians, neither black nor white;

and some of them with red, and some of them with whatever they find. And some of them paint their faces, and some of them the whole body, and some of them only the eyes, and some of them only the nose. They do not carry arms nor are they acquainted with them, because I showed them swords and they took them by the edge and through ignorance cut themselves. They have no iron. Their javelins are shafts without iron and some of them have at the end a fish tooth and others of other things. All of them alike are of good-sized stature and carry themselves well. I saw some who had marks of wounds on their bodies and I made signs to them asking what they were; and they showed me how people from other islands nearby came there and tried to take them, and how they defended themselves; and I believed and believe that they come here from *tierra firme* [the mainland] to take them captive. They should be good and intelligent servants, for I see that they say very quickly everything that is said to them; and I believe that they would become Christians very easily, for it seemed to me that they had no religion. Our Lord pleasing, at the time of my departure I will take six of them from here to your Highnesses in order that they may learn to speak. No animal of any kind did I see on this island except parrots. All are the Admiral's words.

Sunday, 13 October

Document 2. "Everyone was amazed to catch sight of . . . things they had never dreamed or heard": *History of the Indies*, 1493

Las Casas was a great admirer and strong critic of Columbus.[2] As a young boy, he was present at the admiral's first return voyage from the New World. In the spring of 1493, when Columbus slowly made his way across Spain from Seville to court in Barcelona, great wonder and possibilities seemed to fill the air, especially at the court of Isabel and Ferdinand. How does Columbus envision the future task and purpose of a European presence in the Indies? What do the Spaniards, including the king and queen, think and feel about the "discovery" of a New World? What would be a comparable kind of "discovery" in our day and age?

After the courier was dispatched, Christopher Columbus, now the Admiral, dressed in the best attire he could find, departed from Seville taking the Indians with him. There were only seven Indians remaining from the previous hardships, for the others had died. I myself saw them in Seville at that time; they were lodging near the arch called the Arch of Images, by Saint Nicholas. Columbus carried very beautiful green parrots, vibrant in color, and *guaycas*, which were masks made of a collection of fish bone arranged like pearls, and some belts of the same material, fashioned with admirable craftsmanship. He also had a great quantity and variety of very fine gold, and many other things never seen or heard of in Spain.

Columbus hastened from Seville with the Indians and the others. Word began to spread quickly throughout Spain that new lands called "the Indies" had been discovered along with a multitude of exotic people and new things and that the discoverer himself was coming, on this or that road, bringing these people with him. Not only did the world stop to catch a glimpse in the towns he passed through, but even distant villages became vacant as many filled the roads to see for themselves and to go beforehand to the town so that they could join in the welcome reception.

Having received the memorials of Columbus from Seville, the Crown of Ferdinand and Isabel decreed that plans should commence to prepare what was needed for a second voyage. They wrote to Juan Rodríguez de Fonseca, archdeacon of Seville. . . . This Juan de Fonseca, although an ecclesiastical official, later given charge over the Indies by the Crown, was bishop of Bajadoz, Palencia, and finally Burgos, where he died. He was quite the administrator of worldly affairs, especially in gathering soldiers for fleets at sea, which was work more appropriate for Basques than for bishops. For this reason, the Crown would always entrust him with the task of overseeing the sea fleets they assembled. They now ordered him to take charge of preparing a certain number of ships and men, and make certain provisions, among other things, according to the requests given in the Admiral's memorials.

With great composure and prudence Columbus recounted the many blessings God had granted him on his journey under the favor of such Catholic monarchs. He specifically told them, in whatever appeared relevant and timely, about his entire voyage and discovery. He described the grandeur and prosperity of the discovered lands and affirmed the many more yet to be discovered, for at that time he thought Cuba was the mainland. He showed the items he brought that had never been seen. He took out the large sample of gold consisting of fashioned pieces, despite the lack of polish, and many coarse and fine grains that could be extracted from the land. He assured them of the endless supply of such things in those lands and his confidence that it would restore the royal treasury, as if he had already deposited it under his title.

In the same manner, the most precious and considerable treasure were the many Indian peoples of the land, some of whom were present because Columbus had brought them. He described their simplicity, gentleness, bareness, customs, and the disposition and capacity, of those already known, to be brought to the holy Catholic faith. Having heard and profoundly considered all this, the most devoted Catholic monarchs arose and then fell together onto their knees. With their hands raised and their eyes glossed over with tears, they began to give thanks to the Creator from the depths of their hearts. And since the singers of the royal choir were organized and ready, they sang, "We praise You, O God" (*Te Deum laudamus*). The high-pitched sounds of the musical instruments appeared in that very moment to manifest and come into contact with the delights of heaven.

Who could recount the tears that came from the royal eyes and of the many rulers and of the royal household? What rejoicing, what gladness, and what happiness bathed the hearts of all! How they began to motivate each other and resolve in their hearts to go settle these lands and help convert these peoples! Everyone heard and witnessed the esteemed princes, especially the holy Queen Isabel, who, by her words and by the example of her heroic deeds, made it clear to all the principal pleasure and joy of their souls found to be most worthy before the divine presence that had been provided for by the blessing and financial support of the Crown: they had discovered many infidel nations so well disposed that, in short time, would come to know their Creator, and convert to become members of the holy and universal Church. The Catholic faith and Christian religion would thus be vastly expanded.

Immense joys came to the hearts of these blessed monarchs during their reign, even though, as the crown of their merits, God always mixed enough deep sorrows to show his singular care for their betterment. Joys like the birth of the prince, John; to see the cross of Jesus Christ placed in the Alhambra of Granada, when, after such immense hardships, they took that great city and that entire kingdom . . . and other joys that God gave them in this life. But certainly, I have always felt that what they received from this miraculous discovery was not inferior to the other joys, indeed I believe it greatly surpassed them. That is because it was rooted in spirituality: in giving honor and glory to God's name and the wide extension of the holy Catholic faith. The conversion of an infinite number of souls in the large expanse of the New World is far greater than in the reign of Granada, which is limited by the narrow confines of this little corner. The joys caused by God and rooted in the spiritual things of God are more personal and intense. . . .

Finally, the most serene monarchs gave the Admiral permission, for that day, to go rest in his lodgings. At which point he left the whole court under the command of the monarchs and was honorably escorted.

II

The Black Legend

History best remembers Las Casas for recording Spanish brutality in the Conquest of the Indies. Las Casas meant to hold the mirror up to his fellow Spaniards so they would repent and do right by his account—*An Account, Much Abbreviated, of the Destruction of the Indies*. But Spain's European Protestant rivals for empire—especially the English and Dutch—translated the *Destruction of the Indies*, added gory images, and convicted the Spaniards by their own testimony. The Black Legend accused the Spanish of being uniquely cruel and barbaric in the conquest of the Indies as Spain's imperial rivals vied for their own share of trade and settlement outside Europe. This section, presenting documents from various places in the Indies where the Spanish encountered and subjugated Amerindian peoples, is alive with some major controversies in the historiography of the period, the principal one being the creation and validity of the Black Legend.

Document 3. "The Spaniards were guilty of the very same thing they accused the Indians of": *History of the Indies*, ca. 1503–1509

This is Las Casas's account of what he witnessed on Hispaniola, which became the foundation of the Black Legend.[1] Note the tone he takes, addressing the practice of spreading Christianity through war and forced labor. This topic occupies a central theme of Las Casas's voluminous writings on the Indies. On what grounds does Las Casas challenge the behavior of the Spaniards? What were some of the responses of the Amerindians to the demands of the Spaniards? Based on how Las Casas framed these interactions between Amerindians and Spaniards, assume the side of the Amerindians and use Las Casas's arguments to defend yourself.

The worsening of the situation for the Spaniards and the legal creation of the *repartimiento* or *encomienda* of the Indies as solution.

This treats about how the *comendador mayor* [Governor Ovando's military title as a member of the Order of Alcántara, Master Commander] or someone else told the Kings that because of the liberty enjoyed by the Indians by virtue of the instructions given the Master Commander, they [the Indians] fled from talking with the Christians and did not want to work nor could they be indoctrinated [in the faith]. Note how falsely the Kings were fooled since none of the Indians had been given their liberty; they fled [the Spanish] because of the vexations and oppressions inflicted on them; and no one took care to teach them the faith.

When the Master Commander arrived, he saw that bread and flour were just about exhausted and that many of the people who came with him [on his voyage from Spain to Santo Domingo] were beginning to starve, some dying and many more getting sick, and that—because of the instructions he brought given to him by the Kings [Isabel and Ferdinand]—the Indians were free. And without specific orders on this situation, the Master Commander had to decide what to do, [even knowing that] the Kings did not have the power to force the Indians (nor did even God possess that authority, much less the Kings) to work. The Indians on the other hand were in their villages and towns, peaceful, working and taking care of their women and children without offending anyone, serving and obeying their natural lords, as well as some Spaniards who had taken the daughters of some of the lords or other women as maids and wives, and considered they were married to them. But even suffering vexations and anguish, being a humble and patient people, they tolerated these afflictions. Only the province of Higüey, as I wrote above, had rebelled; I also told the cause.

So, the Master Commander, seeing in those times the difficulties, and having brought more people that he could help (and this has always been one of the principle causes for the destruction of these Indies, as is seen: [it should be prohibited] from bringing so many people from Spain), he wrote the Sovereigns [*los reyes*, referring to Queen Isabel and King Ferdinand] a certain letter, once more extolling his prudence and [speaking of his] good and true conscience

which dictated that he write. And . . . I think he did this in error
and much blindness, a point which has escaped few in Castile. And
I say that he wrote, not because I saw it nor did the Kings say so,
other than to say that they were informed, but because in those days
there was no person or people to which the Kings would listen to
decide on things of such importance, other than him.

He wrote, therefore, or the Kings were informed by him or by
others.

The first, because of the liberty given to the Indians, they fled and
separated themselves from having anything to do with the Christians. So, even when [the Christians] wanted to pay them their daily
wages, the Indians did not want to work and roamed around like
vagabonds and were not available to indoctrinate them and convert
them to our holy Catholic faith, etc.

Now we must note (before moving forward) that the liberty
given to them is the one which we truthfully [will] relate, because
they never heard the news that the Kings had given them liberty.
And so they did not flee or separate themselves from the Spaniards as was their right because of the liberty given them, but they
only fled because of the infinite and unrelenting vexations and terrible oppression, done with such ferocity that all the Indians were
terrified and fled, just like chicks and small birds flee and hide when
they see the hawks. This was, and always will be, the reason the Indians flee from the Spaniards, hiding in caves and entrails of the
land. It is not liberty [which they flee from] which was never given
them nor were they ever afforded it after they heard of the Christians. And this is the truth and nothing but the truth. And what
was written to the Kings were damned lies. And with good cause do
the Indians stay away from the Spaniards who promise to pay them
a daily wage. The Spaniards try to lure them back with parties and
many gifts, but the Indians would rather deal with tigers than have
anything to do them.

Number one: What law were they shown conforming to natural
reason by which they may have been convinced and thus feel obliged to leave their homes, their women and children, and travel
fifty or one hundred leagues to work where the Spanish demanded,
even if they were paid a daily wage? Is it by accident or coincidence
that the Admiral [Columbus] and his brother made war on them?
Send them on ships to Castile as slaves? Capture and place in irons
the two major chiefs [rendered as "chiefs" although *reyes* in the text]

of this island, Caonabó, the chief of the Maguana, and Guarionex, of the Vega Real, and then drowned them on the ships? Or the insults and tyrannies inflicted on this island by Francisco Roldán and his followers? I don't think there is one wise or Christian man who would dare affirm that [the Indians were] obliged to labor on the works and haciendas of the Spaniards for one [lousy] day's wage, even less so compelled by natural or divine law.

And the same thing goes for the lame and false excuse of converting them to our Holy Catholic Faith; I tell you the truth, and I swear to it, there was no interest in those days or in succeeding days, nor in years following, to teach them the doctrine and bring them to our faith any more than to teach cattle, horses or other beasts of the fields to become Christians.

And they said more. From all this [Indian resistance] the Spaniards could not find anyone to work in their fields or help them take out the gold on this island, etc.

And the Indians responded that if the Spaniards accused them falsely of not helping them, but wanted productive fields and ranches, then let them work them themselves; and if they wanted to get rich on gold, get ahold of their tools and start digging and taking out the gold themselves, instead of being vagabonds, lazy, and good-for-nothings—which the Indians were not, for they only ate from the sweat of their work, and they obeyed a [heck of a lot] better the second precept that God commanded; and so the Spaniards were guilty of the very same thing they accused the Indians of.

And the Indians were even less obliged to dig for gold, which was only done by the death of many people forced into this intolerable work demanded by the Spaniards. And here too the Kings/ Sovereigns were lied to, telling them that the Indians did not want to help them take out the gold, beating the poor unfortunate Indians with sticks and whips because they didn't hurry, driven by their insatiable appetites for gold to get rich quick.

And supposing that subordinating the Indians was done "to teach them the faith," (something in truth the Spaniards did not do, against the wishes of the Kings to in fact do so), even taking into account that so many Indians had been killed in cruel wars that caused irreparable damage, the Spaniards had the temerity to ask of the Kings that the Indians at least pay something to help in supporting the Spaniards, or at least a portion of the Spaniards on the island, depriving them of their liberty.

This contribution should not have been, since their liberty was stripped away from them, their lords robbed of their lands, their manner of living totally disrupted, turning them over to the Spaniards to serve them totally in the mines and ranches (and this included all, men and women, young people, children, old people, the pregnant and new mothers) as if they were herds of cattle or sheep or other animals.

In the case presented above, if they were obliged to contribute, it should be if possible very moderate and tolerable and without danger to them, to their homes, to their land so as not to diminish them and have them think of the faith as hateful and onerous.

But, because the entrance of the Spaniards on this island was so violent and bloody with so many murders, deaths, and the loss of so many people, with so many injustices, injuries, and assaults that they [the Indians] had little time to recover, and with such scandalous acts done in the name of the faith—which was the excuse given by the Spanish to come and live on this land—never, and in no time in the past, and now, if they were alive, were they obliged to give or contribute one *maravedí*. And I am sure that any person with reasonable intelligence considering the laws of reason, natural law, and divine positive law, and even into account human laws, well understood, will no doubt affirm and sign to.

I wanted to put all this down here, added to this history, these reasons because they are the principal and fundamental ones of this affair and ignorance of them has destroyed all of these Indies.

Document 4. "There I saw such great cruelties": *An Account, Much Abbreviated, of the Destruction of the Indies*, 1542

This document is really the heart of the Black Legend—where Las Casas describes the reactions of the Taíno cacique (chieftain) Hatuey to the invasion of Cuba and other atrocities on the island. Notice Hatuey's identification of the Spanish god with gold, which "they worship and love much."[2] Las Casas speaks directly of what he takes to be the underlying Spanish motive that marked the early conquest on the islands. Las Casas was an eyewitness, which made his testimony more authoritative in a certain sense because of his personal experience. It also made the horror and atrocity before him more unbearable. As a chaplain to the conquest, he received an *encomienda* grant with native laborers, thus marking the beginning of the end of his complicity and participation in violent colonization. Why would Las Casas choose to include the example of Hatuey in this account?

On the Island of Cuba,

In the year 1511, the Spaniards passed on to the island of Cuba, which, as I have said, is as long as from Valladolid to Rome (and where there were once great provinces of people), and they began and ended in the manners spoken of above and many more, and more cruelly. Here there occurred most singular and abominable things.

There was a high cacique and lord, whose name was Hatuey, who had gone from the island of Hispaniola to Cuba with many of his people, fleeing the calamities and inhumane deeds of the Christians, and being at that time on the island of Cuba, and wishing to give certain news to the Indians there that the Christians would be coming on to that island, he gathered many or all of his people, and he spoke to them thus: "You know that I said that the Christians are soon to be coming here, and you have experience of what has happened to lords so-and-so and so-and-so and so-and-so; and how those Christians have used those nations of Haití (which is Hispaniola), and they are now coming here. And do you know perchance why they do this?" And they replied: "O, save that they are by their nature cruel and evil." And he says: "They do it not for that reason alone, but rather because they have a god that they worship and love much, and to make us love him they work to subjugate us and slay us."

He had a small basket nigh beside him [nigh beside him?], filled with gold and gems, and he said: "You see here the god of the Christians: let us do, if you think it right, *areytos* (which are their dances) to him, and perhaps we can please him and he shall command them not to do us harm." And all the Indians there shouted out to him: "That is good, that is good." And they danced before him until they had all wearied, and afterward the lord Hatuey said: "Look, even so, if we keep him, to get him from us they shall surely slay us; let us throw him into this river." And all vowed to do that, and so they threw the basket into the river, a large river that was right there.

This cacique and lord was constantly fleeing from the Christians, from the moment they came to that island of Cuba, being one who knew them well, and he would defend himself when he came upon them, but at last they captured him. And for no reason but that he fled such iniquitous and cruel people, and defended himself from those who wished to slay him and oppress him until the death of him and all his people and the succeeding generations, they burned him alive. And when he was bound to the stake, a friar of

the order of Saint Francis, a holy father was thereby, spoke some
things to him concerning God and our faith, which he had never
heard before—or as much as what that friar was able in the short
time that the executioners gave him—and the friar asked if the lord
wished to believe those things that he told him, for if he did he
would go to the sky (that is, heaven), where there was glory and eternal rest but if not, he would certainly go to hell and suffer perpetual
torments and sufferings. And thinking a while, the lord asked the
holy father whether Christians went to the sky. The priest replied
that they did, but only those who were good. And the cacique then
said without thinking on it any more, that he did not desire to go to
the sky, but rather down to hell, so that he would not be where *they*
were and would not see such cruel people. And this is the fame and
honor that our faith has won by the work of those Christians who
have gone out to the Indies.

Once, some Indians were coming out to us to receive us with
provisions and gifts ten leagues from a great village, and when we
came to them we were given a great quantity of fish and bread and
food and all else that they were able. But suddenly the devil came
upon the Christians, and in my presence they took out their knives
(with no reason or cause that might be alleged in justification) and
slew above three thousand souls who were sitting there before us,
men and women and children. And there I saw such great cruelties
that no living man had ever seen the like of them before or thought
to see.

Another time, a few days thence, I sent messengers to all the
lords of the province of La Habana, assuring them not to fear (for
they had heard of me to my credit), telling them not to absent
themselves but to come out to receive us, that no harm whatsoever
would be done them (for the entire land was stricken with horror
at the slaughters that had been done), and this I did with consent
of the captain. And when we arrived at the province, they did come
out to receive us, some twenty-one lords and caciques, and afterward the captain, in breach of the assurances I had given them, took
hold of them and desired the next day to burn them alive saying
that it was right, because those lords must at some time have committed some act to merit it. And it was most difficult for me to save
them from the pyre, but at last they did escape it.

After all the Indians of the island were cast into the same servitude and calamity as those of Hispaniola, seeing all of themselves
and their people die and perish without any help for it, some began

to flee into the wilderness, others to hang themselves in despera-
tion and lack of hope, and husbands and wives to hang themselves
together, and with them, hang their children. And because of the
cruelties of one most tyrannous Spaniard (whom I met) above two
hundred Indians hanged themselves. An infinite number died in
this manner.

There was an officer of the king upon this island who was given
as *repartimiento* three hundred Indians, and at the end of three
months two hundred and sixty of them had died in the labors of the
mines, so that no more than thirty remained, which was the tenth
part of them. After that, he was given as many more again, or more
even than that, and he also slew these and he would be given more,
and slay more, until at last he died and the devil had his soul.

In the three or four months that I abode there, above seven thousand children starved to death, because their fathers and mothers
had been carried off to the mines. And many other such heinous
things of that kind did I see.

After that, they resolved to go out and search for the Indians
who had fled into the wilderness and the mountains, and there
they wrought terrible havoc and devastation, and so thoroughly laid
waste to all that island and left it uninhabited [deserted], as we ourselves saw not long ago, that it is a great shame and pity to see it
bare and waste and rendered a very desert of solitude.

Document 5. "And so he had them burned alive": *An Account, Much Abbreviated, of the Destruction of the Indies*, ca. 1540s

This selection is from "On the Kingdom and Province of Guatemala" and
describes how the *entrada* (armed expedition) used fear and terror, led by
the conquistador Pedro de Alvarado.[3] The description of the Spaniards is
hard to believe as one reads it, even if one accounts for some exaggeration
and hyperbole that Las Casas built into his accounts to persuade his read-
ers of the events he witnessed. Do you think Las Casas exaggerated his
account? If so, why? What did the people do when they saw their chiefs
burned alive?

On the Province and Kingdom of Guatimala
When he came to that kingdom, as he made his *entrada* he
slaughtered many people. And despite this, there came out to receive him, upon litters and with trumpets and tambors [drums]
and great celebrations, the principal lord with many other lords of

the city of Utatlan, the chief city of the entire kingdom, and they
served him with all that they had, especially giving them victuals
as was meet, and all that they were able. As for the Spaniards, they
made a camp outside the city that night, because it appeared to
them strong and thus that within, there might be danger. And the
day following, he called out the principal lord and many other lords,
and when they had come to him like gentle lambs, he laid hold of
them all and told them that they were to give him so many *cargas*
[loads] of gold. They replied that they had it not, because that land
did not bear gold. And so he had them burned alive, with no further guilt or trial or sentence. And when the lords of all those provinces saw that their supreme lord and the other high lords had all
been burned, and for no reason but that they would not give them
gold, they all fled their villages into the wilderness, and they ordered
all their people, that they go to the Spaniards and serve them as if
they were their masters, but not reveal where they had gone. All
the people of the land came to the Spaniards then and told them
that they belonged to them and that they would serve them as their
masters. This pious captain replied that he would not receive them,
and indeed that he would have them all burned alive unless they revealed where their lords had gone. The Indians said that they knew
not, that he was to employ them as he would, them and their wives
and children, who could be found in their houses, and there they
might slay or do with them as they would, and many times the Indians said this and offered this and did this. And it was a wonder to
see, that the Spaniards went to the villages, where the poor people
were working at their labors with their wives and children safe by,
and there they ran them through with their spears and hacked them
into pieces. And to a very great and powerful village they came (its
people more careless than others and thinking in their innocence
that they were safe) and the Spaniards entered and in a space of
two hours almost razed them to the ground, putting children and
women and old persons to the sword and slaying as many as they
could, who, though fleeing, did not escape.

And when the Indians saw that even with so much humility and
offerings and patience and suffering they still could not break or
soften such inhumane and bestial hearts, and that so without ap-
pearance or color or reason, and indeed so perfectly contrary to it,
they were hacked to pieces, and seeing that they were to die for
no cause and in the very twinkling of an eye, they agreed to meet
and to join together and to die in war, taking vengeance as best

they could upon such cruel and hellish enemies, for they well knew that being not just unarmed, but naked, on foot, and weak, against people so fierce, on horseback and so well armed, they could not prevail, but in the end would be destroyed.

Document 6. "My one motive in dictating this book": Prologue to *History of the Indies*, 1552

This short rationale for writing his *History of the Indies* is a summary of Las Casas's calling as a historian and advocate of the Amerindian cause.[4] Consider the important relationship between the reporting of truth and the pursuit of justice and right. According to Las Casas, what is the role of a historian? In what sense does the writing of history entail moral concerns? How does this early modern historical task compare/contrast with investigative journalism today?

My one motive in dictating this book was that I saw Spain had an urgent, a mortal need to have the truth, the light of the truth shed on Indian affairs, a long-standing need, and at every level of society. For lack of that truth, or the meagerness of it, what huge calamities occurred out in the Indies, what violence, what slaughter of whole peoples, what losses of soul, dead in this life and in the life to come, what massive injustice! And here in the realm of Castile, what frequent and unforgivable sins have been committed, what blindness and stifling of conscience, what pitiful damage was done, is done every day, because of what I just described. What happened will never be revealed as it ought, I am certain, never weighed, assessed, bewailed as it ought, until that last fearsome day of strict and accurate divine judgment. . . .

I know some people have written about Indian affairs, not from what they witnessed, but secondhand and poorly heard (though they don't admit it), and have done deep damage to the truth. . . . So, the seed they sowed was bad, erratic, fruitless, it came from self-seeking, worldly instincts, it ended producing a greater and greater crop of that choking weed in people, increasingly—knowledge that was shockingly false and conscience that was twisted. To such an extent that the Christian faith itself has suffered irreparable damage, and the long-standing moral values of the Church universal as well, and of almost the whole human race. . . .

We are to believe that God has chosen for salvation some from among every single group of human beings and has determined the time of their calling, their conversion, their glorification. But we do not know who they are, those chosen. So, we must think and feel and judge and act and be helpful toward every human being, as if we wanted them to be the saved, and wanted with our works to help effect their salvation insofar as we could and we were sure that everyone was called. . . .

I have thought long and hard and often about the defects, the errors laid out above and the manifest, the harmful things that happened and still happen as a result. And [I have] thought how "right is born and originates from the truthful accounting of reality," so the canon lawyers say.[5] So I decided to write about the major events of the Indies, some of which I saw done, saw happen right before my eyes during my sixty and some years of life—for I was there present, in various areas, realms, provinces, lands—and write also about things public and notorious, not just those over and done with, but also the very many that go on all the time.

III

Slavery and the New Laws

In his unrelenting and sometimes shortsighted defense of Amerindians, Las Casas suggested bringing slaves from either Spain or Africa to lift the burden of oppression off the backs of the Amerindians. He has since then been pilloried by some critics for being one of the "initiators" of the notorious African slave trade. It is important to observe, however, that he later vehemently condemned the slave trade, just as he had done in the case of the Spanish wars of conquest. Although Las Casas was not an abolitionist in the modern sense, he made the justifications for legal enslavement much stricter than his contemporaries did. By the end of his life, he was adamant that the enslavement of both the Amerindians and the Africans had been unjustly committed through false rationales for war. The only legitimate response by the oppressors in the final instance was restoring the victims to their freedom and their livelihood.

Document 7. "Enslavement of blacks was every bit as unjust as that of the Indians": *History of the Indies*, ca. 1550–1560

Las Casas painfully confronts his complicity here of the African slave trade that began in the fifteenth century and led to the rise of sugar plantations in the New World.[1] He includes the violent seizure of black Africans under the Portuguese as recorded by Gómez Eanes de Zurara, a chronicler of Prince Henry "the Navigator" (see Document 22). How did the Portuguese defend their actions in Africa? In what ways were the enslavements of the Amerindians and Africans both similar and different? Describe Las

Casas's process of self-analysis in addressing his earlier actions promoting African slavery.

LAS CASAS CONFESSES AND REPENTS HIS ERROR

1. His early involvement

Some Spaniards on the island contacted the cleric Las Casas. They saw his purpose, saw that the religious of St. Dominic would not absolve those who held Indians unless they gave them up. If he could get them a license from the king so they could import from Castile a dozen blacks, they would free their Indians. The cleric agreed and requested in his reports that the favor should be done [for] the Spanish settlers on the islands, and they each should be given a license to bring in from Spain about a dozen black slaves. The settlers could thus continue to work the land, consequently they would free their Indians. When the cleric Las Casas first gave that advice—to grant the license to bring black slaves to the islands—he was not aware of the unjust ways in which the Portuguese captured and made slaves of blacks. But after he found out he would not have proposed it for all the world, because blacks were enslaved unjustly, tyrannically, right from the start, exactly as the Indians had been.

2. His judgment on himself and on the Spaniards

Before sugar mills were invented, some settlers, who had some wealth they had gotten from the sweat and blood of the Indians, wanted a license to buy black slaves back in Castile. The settlers saw they were killing off the Indians. But they still had some: so they promised the cleric Bartolomé de las Casas that if he succeeded in getting them the license to import a dozen blacks to the island, they would allow the Indians they held to be set free. With this promise in mind, the cleric Las Casas got the king to allow the Spaniards of the islands to bring in some black slaves from Castile so the Indians could then be set free. As we said earlier, Las Casas was in favor with the king who had recently come to power and watch over the new territories that had been put in Las Casas's hands. The council, with the accord of the authorities in Seville, decided that a license should be given to import four thousand black slaves, for starters, to the four islands: Hispaniola, San Juan, Cuba, Jamaica. Sure enough, a Spaniard from the Indies who was then at court found out about the decision and slipped the information to the governor of Bresa— a Flemish gentleman who had come with the king and was of his inner circle—so he could request the franchise. He requested it, he got it, he sold it to the Genoese for twenty-five thousand ducats. The Genoese were shrewd and set a thousand conditions. One was that for eight years no further license be given out to bring black slaves to the Indies. The Genoese then sold individual licenses or individual blacks at eight ducats apiece minimum. Thus, the permission the cleric Las Casas had gotten so the Spaniards could get help in working the land, to free their Indians, was turned into a profit-making scheme. It proved to be a great setback to the well-being and liberation of the Indians. The cleric, many years later, regretted the advice he gave the king on this matter—he judged himself culpable through inadvertence—when he saw proven that the enslavement of blacks was every bit as unjust as that of the Indians. It was not, in any case, a good solution he had proposed, that blacks be brought in so Indians could be freed. And this even though he thought that the blacks had been justly enslaved. He was not certain that his ignorance and his good intentions would excuse him before the judgment of God.

There were at that time only ten or twelve blacks on the island; they belonged to the king, they had been brought in to construct a fortress which overlooked the river mouth. But once the license was given and implemented, others followed and frequently, so eventually thirty thousand blacks were brought to the island [Hispaniola], and I reckon 100,000 to the Indies as a whole. But the traffic did not help or free the Indians. And the cleric Las Casas could not exert further influence—the king was away, the council got new members every day, and were ignorant of law, law they were obliged to know. I have said this often throughout my *History*. As the sugar mills increased daily in number the need to put blacks to work in them also increased; the water-powered ones needed at least eighty; the mechanical ones thirty to forty, so that the profit to the king increased. Something else followed from this situation. The Portuguese had made a career in much of the past of raiding Guinea and enslaving blacks, absolutely unjustly. When they saw we had such a need of blacks and they sold for high prices, the Portuguese speeded up their slave raiding—they are still in a hurry. They took slaves in every evil and wicked way they could. And blacks, when they saw the Portuguese so eager on the hunt for slaves, they themselves used unjust wars and other lawless means to steal and sell to the Portuguese. And we are the cause of all the sins the one and the other commit, in addition to what we commit in buying them.

Document 8. "By what right and with what justice?": *History of the Indies*, 1511

This selection[2] recounts the sermons of the Dominican friar Antonio Montesino, beginning in Advent of December 1511, in the city of Santo Domingo on the island of Hispaniola. In the common spirit of the Dominicans in the New World, Montesino called for the recognition of the Taínos of the island, and all other natives by extension, as humans fully capable of freely converting to Christianity. Montesino's sermons were the first summons to justice and rights in the Americas and stand as a hallmark in the history of Christianity in the New World. What teachings and practices does Montesino employ to challenge and change the behavior of the Spaniards toward the Taínos? How do the Dominicans respond to Spanish colonial backlash?

When it came to the time to preach on Sunday, Father Antonio Montesino ascended the pulpit and took as the theme and basis for his sermon that which was written and signed by the other friars: *Ego vox clamantis in deserto* ("I am a voice crying in the desert"). After his introduction and saying something about the season of Advent, he began to emphasize the arid desert of consciences among Spaniards of the island and the blindness in which they lived; also, in what danger of eternal damnation they were in for taking no heed of the grave sins in which, with such apathy, they were entrenched and dying.

Then he turned to the theme saying: "I have come here to make you aware. I am the voice of Christ in the desert of this island. It would be wise of you to pay attention and to listen with your whole heart and with every fabric of your being. This voice will be new and unlike anything you have ever heard. It will be the harshest and difficult, and the most frightful and dangerous; one that you never would have imagined hearing." This voice cried out for some time with very combative and incriminating words making everyone's flesh tremble as if they were standing before the judgment of God.

In epic fashion the voice, beseeching all, then declared what was at stake in the message: "This voice," he said, "declares that you are all in mortal sin. You live in it; you die in it. All because of the cruel tyranny you exercise against these innocent peoples. Tell me, by what right and with what justice do you so violently enslave these Indians? By what authority do you wage such hideous wars against these people who peacefully inhabit their lands, killing infinite numbers of them by unimaginable and unspeakable means? How can you oppress them giving neither food nor medicine and by working them to death all for your insatiable thirst for gold?

"And what care do you provide them spiritually in teaching them about their God and creator, so they are baptized, hear mass, and keep holy days? Are they not human beings? Do they not have rational souls? Are you not obligated to love them as you love yourselves? Do you not understand or feel this? How can you remain so profoundly asleep and indifferent? Surely, you are no better suited for salvation than the Moors and Turks who neither have nor want the Christian faith."

Finally, the voice explained what it had implored before in such a manner that it left them astonished—many were indifferent and without feeling, others became even more obstinate, while some felt a bit of guilt. But none of them, which I later learned, were converted.

When Montesino had concluded the sermon, he descended from the pulpit with his head not at all low because he was a man who did not want to show fear. Even if he had given much displeasure to his listeners for having said and done what was suitable to him according to God, he did not fear. With his companion he went to his thatched house, where, luckily, they had nothing to eat but cabbage broth with no olive oil, as sometimes happened. After departing, the church remained full of murmurs, which, I believe they hardly let the Mass finish. . . .

After the friars were done eating, which must not have tasted so well, the whole city gathered at the Admiral's house, where his son, Diego Columbus, was specifically gathered with the king's officials—the treasurer, the auditor, the broker, and the controller. They agreed to go confront and scare the preacher and the others, if not to punish him as a scandalous man for introducing a new doctrine never before heard condemning everyone. He said against the king and his regime in the Indies that they could not possess the Indians, which had been given them by the king. For it was a grave and unpardonable matter to say such things.

They called the porter who opened the door. They told him to summon the Vicar, and the friar who had preached such ravings. Only the Vicar, the venerable Father Fray Pedro de Córdoba, came out. They told him with more haughtiness than humility to summon the one who had preached. Córdoba responded with great prudence by telling them it was unnecessary to do so. Since he was the authority over the religious, he would respond to whatever the Admiral and his graces needed. They strongly insisted that he call upon the preacher. But Córdoba, with such wisdom and authority, deflected them with humble yet firm words, as was his manner of speaking. Divine Providence had gifted him with those virtues naturally acquired. He was a person deeply honored and pious whose very presence garnered the most profound respect.

When the Admiral and the others realized that the Vicar was not persuaded by their reasons and words resting on authority, they began to ease up their strong language. They beseeched Córdoba to summon the preacher so that they could ask him on what basis had he decided to preach something so new and offensive that was a disservice to the king and harmful to everyone in the city and on the island. After the holy friar sensed they had taken a different tack and their passions had abated since their arrival, he called for Antonio Montesino. The fear be damned with which he came. When everyone was seated, the Admiral spoke first by presenting his complaint and that of the others. How could this priest boldly preach things that were so contrary to the king and against everyone on the island by suggesting that the Spaniards could not possess the Indians? For they had been given by the king, who was lord of all the Indies, especially after the Spaniards had gained the islands with great labor and had conquered the infidels who held them. Since the sermon was so scandalous and of such great disservice to the king and offensive to the people of the island, they had decided that the priest should retract everything he had said. Otherwise, they would supply an appropriate remedy.

The Vicar responded to them by saying that what had been preached by the priest had been the opinion reached willingly by unanimous consent of everyone, including himself. They had achieved this after examining the matter closely among themselves. Following much counsel and mature deliberation, they had decided to preach as the true Gospel what was necessary for the salvation of the Spaniards and the Indians on the island. They witnessed the latter perishing daily and being treated with no more care than the beasts of the field. The friars were obligated to do so by the divine precept they had professed in baptism, first as Christians and then as vowed preachers of the truth. They did not see themselves as causing disservice to the king, who, after all, had sent them here to preach whatever they sensed was necessary for souls. Rather, they intended to serve him with complete loyalty, and they were certain that once His Highness was well informed of what was really happening here, and about what they had preached, he would consider himself served well and would give them his thanks.

The explanation and reasons given by Córdoba justifying the sermon were of little use in pleasing and calming the anger prompted in those who heard that they could not hold the Indians as they did in such a tyrannical way to satisfy their greed. If the Indians were taken from them, they would be cheated of all their desires and their hopes. It followed that each one of them present, especially the authorities, said what was favorable to their purpose.

They all agreed that Father Montesino should recant the following Sunday what he had preached; and they reached such a level of blind ignorance that they said that if he did not do so, the friars should collect their straw huts and return to Spain.

The Vicar replied: "Certainly, lords, we can do so with very little effort." And this was truly the case since their valuables were nothing more than coarsely stitched habits and some blankets made from the same material for sleeping. . . . Seeing how unfazed the servants of God were by every manner of threat made against them, the officials toned it down, beseeching them to reevaluate the matter; and, after deeper consideration, to emend in another sermon what was previously stated to satisfy the community, which was greatly scandalized.

Finally . . . the friars conceded, in their effort to be done with the officials, and conclude such frivolous nuisances, said they would in good time send the same Father Montesino the following Sunday to preach and return to the subject matter that he previously preached about. And that he would try to satisfy the community as much as possible regarding everything that was said. With this agreement, the officials left pleased and hopeful.

Some of the officials later printed what had been agreed upon by them and the Vicar and that the following Sunday the friar would renounce everything that he had said the week before. . . . When the time came for the sermon, [with Montesino] at the pulpit, the text serving as the basis for his retraction was from the Book of Job (36:3): "*I will repeat my knowledge from the beginning*, and I will prove my sermon to be without falsehood." In other words, "I will reconsider once again from the beginning the knowledge and the

truth that I preached to you last Sunday, and I will demonstrate
the truthfulness of that which embittered you." Having heard this,
the most perceptive among the listeners knew exactly where he was
going, and it was total misery to let him continue. He began his sermon and referred to everything that he previously preached and to
defend with even more reasons and authorities what he declared:
that those broken and oppressed peoples were held unjustly and tyrannically. He went back to repeating his conviction that the Spaniards would certainly not be saved in such a state, and that they
should be healed in due time. He let them know that the friars
would refuse to hear confessions from any of them, any more than
they would hear the confession of one in the act of robbing another.
And that any of them can publish and write this to whomever they
wished in Castile since the friars believed with great certainty that
they were serving God and offering no small service to the king.

Once the sermon was finished, Father Montesino returned home,
and the entire town in the church remained there agitated, and
much angrier with the friars than before. They found themselves
denuded of their vain and wicked hope that what was said would
be unsaid—as if the law of God against which they oppressed and
crushed these peoples, could be changed.

Document 9. "The preservation . . . of the Indians, has always been the primary purpose of our policy": New Laws of 1542, Council of the Indies[3]

The New Laws were issued by Emperor Charles V upon the recommenda-
tion of a special commission he called to review the laws governing the Indies.[4] Las Casas appeared before this commission almost literally night and
day, and his testimony and recommendations became the basis of the New
Laws. What policies toward the *encomienda* and conquest did the New
Laws specifically stipulate? Do you think the New Laws were a legitimate
expression of the royal will, or just palliatives to satisfy critics like Las Casas and his supporters?

Laws, Regulations, and General Policies

Since the preservation and welfare of the Indians have always
been the primary purpose of our policy, we order our Council to
pay close attention to, and to take special care concerning, the
safety, good government, and treatment, of the Indians. We order

the Council to ensure that the Indians receive instruction in matters concerning our Catholic faith, and that they be well treated as our vassals and the free peoples that they are. The Council should be aware of everything concerning the special care, preservation, and good government of our Indians, and comply with and execute our orders for the good government of our Indies, including the administration of justice, and to ensure that all laws are obeyed faithfully and without failure.

Since one of the major responsibilities of the Audiencias [High Courts] in our service is to watch very carefully over the good treatment and safety of the Indians, we order them to constantly keep informed of violations and the bad treatments which have been inflicted or continue to be inflicted on the Indians by governors or private individuals. And to see that these same people have observed the rules and regulations they were given concerning the good treatment of the Indians.

And in cases where there is violation, now or in the future, the Audiencias should correct the situations, punishing the culprits severely within the limits of the law. And they should not allow postponements of juridical cases between Indians or against them to drag on forever. This usually happens due to the malice of some lawyers and prosecutors. Instead, the cases shall be determined expediently in accord with Indian custom and usage provided these are not clearly unjust. And the Audiencias should see to it that lower court judges be just as efficient and just.

On the Prohibition of Indian Slavery

Item: And we order that from this day forward, no Indian may be enslaved for any reason whatsoever, even if the Indians were in rebellion or holding Spaniards as hostages or in any other way. And we want the Indians to be treated as our vassals, since that is what they are.

No one may use Indians as *naboría*, nor *tapia*, nor in any other way against their will.[5]

And since we have ordered that from here on no Indians may be enslaved, and we have included those who against reason and law have been enslaved against the provisions and instructions already in place, we order the Audiencias to free those Indians immediately based on an honest appraisal of the truth, if those people who held Indians in slavery have no legal or legitimate title. And we instruct

the Audiencias to put people of confidence in charge of defending
the Indian cause and that they dispose of their charge diligently and
that they be paid out of the fines adjudged.

Prohibiting Royal and Ecclesiastical Officials from Holding Indians in Encomienda

There has been much detriment in the treatment of the Indians
because they are held by viceroys and governors, their lieutenants
and our officials, and by prelates, monasteries and hospitals, houses,
people connected with houses of religion, our treasury officials,
and other people favored because of their offices. It is our wish and
command that all these Indians forthwith be put directly under
our Royal crown [and taken away] from viceroys, governors, vice-
governors, officials of any kind such as of justice and of the treasury, prelates, houses both religious and civil, hospitals, confrater-
nities and the such, even if the Indians had not been awarded to
them because of their offices. And even if the officials and governors
desired to renounce their offices and governorships to enable them
to keep the Indians, do not allow this or anything else to block our
command.

Prohibition of the Encomienda

And the Audiencias should investigate and inform themselves
on how Indians have been treated by people who hold them in encomiendas. And if the Indians have been abused and badly treated,
then the encomenderos should be stripped of their Indians and
those Indians be put under our royal crown.

And we also order that from now on no new encomiendas be
awarded or created for whatever reason. And as encomenderos die,
their Indians be placed under our royal crown. And that the Audiencias see to it that the wife and children of the deceased encomenderos be properly taken care of by a modest amount of tributes col-
lected from the Indians as the Audiencias see fit.

On the Just Treatment of the Indians

And we order that our presidents and judges of the Audiencias
take great care that the Indians removed from the encomenderos be
well treated and instructed in the things of our Holy Catholic Faith
as the free vassals which they are. And this responsibility should
be the primary responsibility of those entrusted with the Indians
and we shall judge them accordingly. And they should see that the

Indians are governed with justice like those under our royal crown are being treated presently in New Spain [Mexico].

Regulations for Future Explorers and Discoverers

In future provisions for exploration and discoveries we order: that no Indians be taken from anywhere—the islands or the Mainland—even if they are said to have been sold to them as slaves, on pain of death. Only three or four may be taken as interpreters, even though others may volunteer to come freely. Nothing may be done against the will of the Indians except for legitimate, unforced trade, and this should be overseen by a person named by the Audiencia. And the discoverers should keep all the orders and instructions received from the Audiencia, on pain of having all their goods taken away.

Protecting the Indians of Cuba, Hispaniola, and Puerto Rico

And we order that the Indians who live on the islands of San Juan [Puerto Rico], Cuba, and Hispaniola, for now and in the future, not be required to pay tributes or render other royal taxes either personally or as a group other than those which Spaniards are required to render on those islands. And that the Indians be allowed to enjoy peace and liberty so that they may multiply and be instructed in the things of our Holy Catholic Faith.

Document 10. "For everyone to accept our faith, he or she must have . . . a clear liberty of choice": *Twenty Reasons against the Encomienda*, 1552

In this treatise published in 1552, Las Casas provides one of his earliest and most comprehensive arguments against the forced labor institution of the *encomienda* by defending the principle of Amerindian freedom.[6] This defense illustrates how Las Casas subsumed everything under the spiritual mission to convert the peoples of the New World in a peaceful manner. If the Spaniards did anything to compromise that supreme goal, then they would lose the privilege entrusted to them by the Roman Church. Pope Alexander VI's *Inter caetera* (1493) provided the legal and spiritual rationale for ongoing Spanish presence in the Americas. Which actions specifically undermine or negate freedom? What is the political and spiritual significance of liberty in this document?

Take it as true, then, that the peoples and places of the New World are free. They are obligated to no one in any way for anything before they are discovered, during their discovery, today after their discovery—save only to Your Majesty, a service, an obedience, a specific kind, the kind free people and places owe their supreme king and Lord. Take it as true also, the special condition of these peoples which makes them even freer than other peoples, i.e. that the Kings of Castile have no claim to these peoples. They are not an inheritance, not a purchase, not an exchange. They were not conquered in a just war motivated by the just cause of having harmed Spain, or the universal Church, or any member of it, or summoned to make restitution or satisfaction and been unwilling to do so. They were not squatters in bad faith on some territory. They did not harbor stolen goods, with no intention of giving them back. No such circumstances.

The fact is that these peoples will accept of their own free will the supreme Lordship of Your Majesty. If they have not accepted our Kings in the past, the reason has been that no one up to now has asked them to, nor given them the chance to be asked, nor considered them as worth more than the animals they beat the bush for. The Indians have seen no just or sound reason why they should accept Your Majesty. They have no knowledge of Your Majesty's grandeur, your justice, your liberality, your goodness, your power, nor that of your [predecessors] in Castile. Rather, they know widespread violence, insult, tyranny, injustice, cruelty, criminal acts done by Spaniards. That is why the Indians think so badly of Your Majesty and your predecessors, all the Kings of Castile. They have good reason, though you have not deserved what they think. They have a mortal hatred of Your Majesty, a horror toward your whole lineage. They think Their Highnesses, as Your Majesty, know and consent to, foster and urge that they be treated just as I described.

Furthermore, note the title which Their Highnesses and Your Majesty hold, the apostolic mission granted by the Holy Apostolic See. It is the basis for your entire authority over the New World. It states the goal the Kings promised to seek voluntarily, the preaching of the faith in the Indies, the announcement of the Holy Gospel of Jesus Christ, to convert the natives to it. And that is a privilege for the Indians' sake primarily, as I said earlier, not so much for Your Majesty's. The privilege requires great prudence, great control and moderation, great gentleness and kindness, both in early dealings with those peoples, exploring their kingdoms peacefully, lovingly, on best behavior, and later in governing them and in dealing with local Indian populations for whom the place is their birthright where they live and are. The purpose is to have them receive our holy faith freely and without odium, so that they may be formed and fashioned and fitted to the Christian religion. The further reason is that no occasion great or small be given for them to curse the name of our God and thus thwart the attainment of salvation. They should love Your Majesty and Kings of Castile. They should praise God with delight for having given them such a just, kind, king and lord of all, whose rule makes the condition they are in now a condition of greater freedom and power associated with free men.

For everyone to accept our faith, he or she must have what faith calls for in a beginner, a clear liberty of choice. God has left it to the responsible free will of each person to accept or reject the faith. And just as the final state which God promises in the whole process has to be based, is based on the free will of those people called, not on coercion or any violence one can inflict on them, so, without any doubt, most noble Lord, the means to that final state must not be against their will—if the means are be kept orderly and just—but rather must accord with it, must have approval and consent of the converted. To show that this is the way it must be done, there are rules and gospel and commandments and strictures which God imposed, the Lord of all creation whose authority everyone must obey.

It is clear that no power on earth has the right to reduce the liberties of innocent people without tossing away the key to justice. Liberty is the highest, the most precious of the temporal goods of the earth. It is cherished early by all creatures from the least to the most aware, above all by rational beings. It is an extremely protected right in any law, as even the laws of our own realm make clear. They oblige us to judge for liberty in doubtful cases, not against it. . . . Free men will not accept any impairment of their freedom, unless it comes from their free choice and not from force. Anything that happens apart from choice is force—violent, unjust, perverse, null and void according to the natural law, since it means making free beings into slaves. There is no greater harm [to life] than this except for death itself. If you cannot take the goods of free and innocent people away from them justly against their wills, much less can you plunder them, rob them of their state of free human being, usurp their liberty. This is beyond comparison to any value or reputation. If a father cannot put a child up for adoption against the wishes of the child, even should the adoption be for the benefit of the child who might thus inherit all (or at least the statutory quarter) of the wealth of the adopting parent, then surely the king cannot transfer or donate his subjects to a lesser lord, stripping them of their relationship to the crown. The parental power a father has over a child is a more ancient one, a more fundamental one. It is of nature and absolutely necessary. It is not based on the consent of the child but on the structure and force of nature itself. The power of a king over his subjects, developed more recently and by the law of nations, is based on the free consent of subjects, and thus does not have the force of nature or absolute necessity. . . .

Lastly, it is a general rule that a prince cannot do anything which would bring harm to his people unless his people consent. I see Your Majesty, out of a sense of justice and rightness, following the custom set by the Catholic Kings, your grandparents, and acting every day to convoke a general assembly and summoning representatives to come to it. And so, I am arguing that to grant the Indians to the Spaniards in encomienda, or as hereditary serfs, or as anything else, would be a servitude so harmful, so gross, so outlandish, so horrible, that it would ruin them, would debase them from their state of being free and human in teeming cities, to a state of decimated cities and abject enslaved beings—not only that, but to the condition of brute beasts. And it does not stop until the Indians are dissolved like salt in water and disappear totally in death, as I said earlier. It makes obvious sense to say this could not, cannot be done to them without their consent, without each one of them submitting to the servitude by their own free wills. In addition, not only is such subjection and alienation contrary to right reason, to natural law and justice, contrary to charity, it is also a despotic and cruel imposition; it is horrible. That is very clear from what I said earlier! Such treatment is equally against God and God's law. It is a shameful insult to God's holy faith, a choking of it, a harsh attack on it, because it keeps the faith stunted and not growing as it should among those peoples. It stifles the preaching of the law of the Gospel. The Son of God said the opposite: "Let this Gospel be preached in the whole world" [Matthew 24:14]. He ordered it in the strictest, most binding sort of command, that the Gospel should be preached under pain of mortal sin and eternal damnation: "Go into the whole world, preach the Gospel to every creature" [Mark 16:15]. "Go forth, teach all nations" [Matthew 28:19]. What is more, such treatment leads to the total, absolute ruin of all those communities, to the complete depopulation of the New World. It is Your Majesty's duty to watch over it, shelter it carefully, defend it, and preserve it. The care is called for by the divine law of charity and love of neighbor, as befits a Christian prince. The preservation is called for by the charge, the mission imposed on you by the Vicar of Christ's command. Therefore, all the sufferings, all the deaths among the Indians result in damage to, in the loss of honor and revenue for both the royal crown and the royal coffers.

Hiſpani cum mulieribus quas in caſtris & balneis ſu-
perato Atabaliba repererunt, libidinem ſuam explent.

A P T O *eAtabaliba, &relata tam inſigni, (nullum enim ſuorum Pizarrus a-
miſit) de Indis victoria, Hiſpani, de tanta prada, & adeo potente Rege ſupera-
to ſibi plurimum gratulantes, totam illam noctem partim genio, partim quieti
indulſerunt, valde enim erant fatigati, nec integro illo die cibum ſumpſerant.
Poſtridie in vicina vrbi Caxamalca loca excurſiones faciunt, & inuentas in
balneis, vno miliari à Caxamalca diſtantibus, mulieres rapiunt, atque cum illis, perinde atq,
cum aliis quas in Atabaliba caſtris repererant, libidinem ſuam explent: Scribunt autem
rerum in India occidentali geſtarum Hiſtorici, repertas fuiſſe cum in
illis balneis, tum Atabaliba caſtris, ad quin-
quies mille feminas.*

C   Atabaliba

Figure 1. An imagined, and idyllic, scene of the earliest contacts between Spaniards and
native Americans. Both bare breasts and soldiers are prominent in the scene, metaphors
for some of the illusions and realities of the conquest that Las Casas faced. Colorized
engraving by the Dutch Protestant artist Theodor de Bry, c. 1590s.

Figure 2. The Black Legend as depicted by Theodor de Bry in the late sixteenth century. The cruel forms of torture are astonishing, and the flames rising in the right background perhaps were intended to symbolize the flames of Hell. From *Regionum indicarum per Hispanos olim devastatarum accuratissima descriptio, insertis figuris æneis ad vivum fabrefactis* (1664).

Figure 3. Nicaragua historian Clemente Guido with the statue *Indians Resisting Oppression*, Old Leon, Nicaragua, July 2004. Note Spanish war dog with jaws on Indian's ankle. Photograph by Lawrence A. Clayton.

Figure 4. "Depiction of Spanish Atrocities Committed in the Conquest of Cuba in Las Casas's 'Brevisima relación de la destrucción de las Indias,'" one of the many depictions of Spanish cruelty in the conquest period. This rendering is by Joos van Winghe based on the original by Theodor de Bry, 1665, based on the Latin edition of 1598 (original, 1552).

Figure 5. Painting of Las Casas in old age, presumably in the decade before his death in 1566. Image courtesy of Padre Aristonico Montero Galban, O.P.

Figure 6. Las Casas still figures prominently in official images in many Latin American countries such as Cuba, Guatemala, and Mexico. This image depicts a coin struck in his honor in Guatemala in 1964. Photo by David M. Lantigua.

Figure 7. Statue of Las Casas in his hometown of Seville, Spain. Photo by Hispalois. Wikimedia Commons: CC-BY-SA-4.0.

Figure 8. Constantino Brumidi's 1876 painting shows an Indian companion with Las Casas as the latter writes a denunciation of the Spaniards' treatment of native Americans. The painting hangs in the Senate wing of the Capitol. Source: Architect of the Capitol.

IV

The Theory and Practice of Peaceful Evangelization

After the moral and spiritual decision to abandon the *encomienda* in 1514, Las Casas began his lifelong commitment to Amerindian advocacy. His ethic of peaceful evangelization was at the heart of this endeavor. Any activity on the part of Spaniards that threatened the spiritual aim of sharing the Good News was considered wrong and unjust. According to the friar Las Casas, evangelization presupposed the free reception of the Gospel without the use of violence and coercion. Due to the instruments of war, enslavement, and pillaging, the Spaniards had undermined this great privilege to evangelize entrusted by Pope Alexander VI. His encounters with King Charles never failed to reiterate this point. Las Casas was not merely a writer and thinker; he was also a preacher, bishop, and advocate. In 1533, practicing what he preached, he intervened peacefully to resolve a potential rebellion between a native cacique named Enriquillo and Spanish authorities.

Document 11. "Our Christian religion is equal for all . . . and does not deprive any of their liberty": *History of the Indies*, 1527–1561

These two documents recount the exchanges between the Bishop of Darien Juan de Quevedo [spelled "Cabedo" by Las Casas] and Las Casas at the court in Barcelona in 1519.[1] In the first document, Las Casas meets up with Quevedo, the first bishop to the Panama region (Darién), knowing that Quevedo had grown wealthy from his participation in the conquest of the region. In the second reading, Las Casas appears before the court and King Charles, and although observing the formalities, Las Casas speaks directly to the king. What reasons does Las Casas present before the king for the great losses suffered by Amerindian peoples? What is the meaning of "nature" in his arguments supporting Amerindians against his Spanish colonialist opponents like Bishop Quevedo?

3. Confrontation between the cleric Casas with the Bishop of Tierra Firme, named El Darién, fray Juan Cabedo

Chapter 147

[This describes when—the Court being still in Barcelona—fray Juan Cabedo, first Bishop of Darién, arrived, and the first confrontation he had with the cleric Casas is described.]

. . . One day the said Bishop of Tierra Firme came to the palace which was the first that the cleric Las Casas heard of the Bishop's arrival. Since the cleric saw him in the King's dining quarters, he asked who this most reverend friar was, and he was told he is a Bishop from the Indies. Las Casas approached him and said: "Sir, because of what I know of the Indies I feel obliged to kiss your hands."

The Bishop asked Juan de Sámano, who later became Secretary of the Indies, with whom am I talking to? "Who is this father?"

Sámano responded, "Sir, that is the gentleman Casas."

The Bishop, with an arrogant flip of his hand, said, "Oh, Mister Casas, and what sermon do you bring to preach to us?"

Casas responded, in no way intimidated, his color rising. "For sure, sir, I have been waiting days to hear you preach, but I also have a pair of sermons prepared for you which, if you want to hear them, I assure you are worth more than all the money you brought back from the Indies."

To which the Bishop responded, "You are lost! You are lost!"

Sámano said, "Sir, with regards to Casas, and his intentions, all these gentlemen present are approving." Sámano said this about the Council [meeting with the King].

The Bishop added a word most uncharacteristic of bishops, that the road to hell is paved with good intentions.

Having heard this old cliché, the cleric, angry, decided to respond to this fool's folly so that those close by could hear. They opened the door to the King's chamber, where the Council was meeting, but out came the Bishop of Badajoz, who was waiting for the Bishop of Tierra Firme so they could go dine together, and so the cleric missed his chance to tongue lash the Bishop with his answer.

Seeing that Cabedo was going to dine with the Bishop of Badajoz and knowing he could damage [Las Casas's] causes, since the Bishop of Badajoz held much favor with the King, and until then the King have much favored the cleric, the cleric decided to go to the castle where the Bishop of Badajoz resided and was having supper.

It happened that the Admiral of the Indies, the second one, Diego Columbus, was also dining there, as well as don Juan de Zúñiga the brother of the Count of Miranda, who later was tutor of the king don Philip when he was prince. And, while dining, the Bishop of Badajoz and the Admiral passed the time playing a game of chess while waiting for the hour to go to the Palace.

About this time the cleric showed up. And as he watched the game, a certain person who had been on this island [Española-Hispaniola] was talking with the bishop of Tierra Firme and said that wheat had been grown on this island. The bishop of Tierra Firme said it wasn't possible. Now, it happened that the cleric had a few sprigs of wheat in his bag [pocket] that had grown in the shade of the orange grove of the monastery of Santo Domingo of this city [Santo Domingo].

The cleric said, with all humility and deference, "For sure, sir, I have seen good wheat grown on that island," and with that, he pulled out a few wheat grains: "See, I have some with me."

The bishop, when he heard the cleric talk, grew irritated, and told him indignantly, "What do you know! This is like the affairs you deal in! You don't know what you're doing!"

The cleric responded quietly. "Are the things I do evil or unjust?"

To which the bishop shot back, "What do you know? And what titles and degrees do you have that you dare speak as you do on these affairs?"

Then the cleric, a little bolder, looking always not to anger the Bishop of Badajoz, responded: "You know, sir, Bishop, how little I know of the business I bring [before the Court]. But even with the few titles you think I have—and I suspect I have even fewer than you think—examine my work and my actions and you will know what I propose to do.

"And the first is that you have sinned a thousand times a thousand by not having put your spirit into saving your sheep and so freed them from the hands of those tyrants destroying them. And the second conclusion is that you ate the flesh and drank the blood of your own sheep. The third is that if you don't make restitution for everything you brought from over there, to the last drop, you can no more be saved than Judas [Iscariot]."

Seeing that he could not win an argument against the cleric, he began to make fun of him, mocking and laughing at the stinging accusations. The cleric, having right on his side, said, "Laughing sir? You should be crying for the unhappiness of your sheep."

The bishop responded, "Yes, here I have tears in my bag," to which the cleric shot back, "I know well that the tears of remorse are a gift of God, and you should beg God for those, not the joking ones of humor, but true tears from the heart to recognize the disgrace and misery of your sheep."

The Bishop of Badajoz remained silent through all of this, playing the game of chess, apparently pleased with what he was hearing. The cleric took some comfort from this, confounding the bishop [Cabedo] and his insensitivity, and was [ready to stop his accusations] at the first word of the bishop of Badajoz, not wanting to anger him or lose his favor.

After what was said, the bishop of Badajoz interrupted the argument, saying, "No more, no more."

Then the Admiral and don Juan de Zúñiga spoke in favor of the cleric Casas, the Admiral referring to the works of and good favor the cleric enjoyed, of which he knew, and don Juan de Zúñiga, having heard of the cleric's good works and intentions.

Then, the cleric being satisfied and quieted, left and went to his quarters.

Chapter 149

[This refers to what the cleric Casas and the Franciscan friar and the second Admiral don Diego Columbus said in the dispute.]

The bishop [Quevedo] finished talking and Monsieur Xevres and the Grand Chancellor stood up and approached the King ceremoniously. Then, returning to his seat, the Chancellor spoke to the cleric. "Micer [what *monsieur* sounded to Las Casas] Bartolomé, His Majesty asks you to speak."

Then the cleric, removing his biretta and making a reverent bow, began in this manner.

"Most powerful and high king and lord. I am one of the original settlers who went to the Indies and have spent many years there. I have not read histories and accounts which may be false and lying but have touched with my own hands and seen with my own eyes immense and inhumane cruelties committed on these peaceful, gentle people never done even in past generations by cruel and irrationally barbarous men. And these were done to them in the Indies without cause or reason, but only from the greed, the insatiable thirst and hunger for gold by our people.

"This was done in two ways. One, by terribly cruel and unjust wars done without cause against them [living peacefully] on their lands and in their homes, in countless numbers of people and towns. The other, after killing the principal lords and leaders, reducing them to servitude—dividing the people by the hundred and by the fifty among themselves [the Spaniards]—throwing them into the mines, where in the end, where they all died from suffering in extracting gold. All these people died from these two causes wherever the Spaniards went (and one of these committing these tyrannies was my own father, although now gone).

"Seeing all this I was moved, not because I was a better Christian than others, but because of a natural compassion from having to witness such great afflictions and injustices suffered by these people who never deserved such treatment. And so, I returned to these kingdoms [Castile, Aragon, etc.] to tell the Catholic king [Ferdinand], your grandfather.

"I found his Majesty in Placencia and told him what I had seen, and he received me graciously and promised to right these wrongs in Seville where he was headed [for the winter]. Afterward he died in route to Seville. And so my plea had no effect, nor did his royal promise come to pass.

"After his death, I spoke with the regents, the Cardinal of Spain, don fray Francisco Ximenes [de Cisneros] and Adrian [co-ruling with Cardinal Cisneros] who is now cardinal of Tortosa, who put into effect everything needed to bring all these persecutions to an end and stop the killing and decimation of these people. But the Spaniards sent to execute these orders and root out the evil failed to do so.

"I thought about all this and after Your Majesty arrived I presented this to him. And all of this would have been fixed if the grand chancellor, the first in Zaragoza, had not died. So, I continue to work on this [getting justice and stopping the killing], but there is no lack of ministers of the enemy, even of virtue and goodness, who, nonetheless are the cause of continuing deaths, because they are taking care of their own interests.

"It is important for Your Majesty to recognize this and take measures to remedy the wrongs. Even leaving aside what this means for your soul, none of your kingdoms, and those adjoining them, are equal in the least bit to the nations and goods on the whole earth. And in telling Your Majesty of all this, I am sure I am doing the greatest favor for Your Majesty that any vassal can do for his prince. I didn't travel to the New World thinking that I was going to serve the King (even while a loyal subject in all respects) but always thinking and believing that I could serve God in a great way, and with much sacrifice.

"But since God is a jealous guardian of his honor, all creatures owe him honor and glory. I can't move a step forward in these issues—which I only took on because of Him—which will bring inestimable goods and services to Your Majesty.

"And to rectify what I speak of, I must say and affirm that I renounce whatever award or worldly prize that Your Majesty may want me to have. And, I ask that if in some time, I or another on my behalf ask *directly* or *indirectly* [emphasis in original], that Your Majesty should not credit me with anything, so that I may not be accused of lying or falsifying to my king and lord.

"And furthermore (most powerful lord), the new world is filled to spilling over with people capable of accepting the Christian faith, and who possess good and virtuous habits by reason and doctrine, and *by nature* [emphasis in original] are free, and they have their kings and natural lords who govern them.

"And as for what the reverend bishop said: that they are *by nature* [emphasis in original] subjagates, as the Philosopher [Aristotle] said in the beginning of his *Politics*; that "those who are innately wise are naturally rulers and masters; and those who are deficient in reason are naturally slaves," well the intention of the Philosopher and the interpretation of the reverend bishop are as different as heaven and earth.[2] And even if it were as the reverend bishop affirms, the Philosopher was a gentile and is burning in hell. And, anyhow, we are only to use his doctrines when it conforms to our holy Catholic faith and customs.

"Our Christian religion is equal for all and is applicable to all nations of the world and it treats all the same and does not deprive any of their liberty nor their lords, nor casts anyone into servitude, on the pretext that they are slaves *by nature* or free, as the reverend bishop indicates.

"And so it is very right for Your Majesty, at the beginning of your reign, to throw out of your kingdom in the Indies these enormous and horrible tyrants who, before God and man, have caused such evil and irreparable harm to a huge part of humankind, so that our Lord Jesus Christ, who died for these people, and your royal Estate prosper for many years."

That was what the cleric Casas spoke, in a speech that lasted three quarters of an hour, and the king and all hung on his every word.

Document 12. "The one and only way": *The Only Way of Attracting All Peoples to the True Religion*, ca. 1534

This document from *The Only Way* summarizes Las Casas as a peaceful missionary priest and strong critic of the Spanish conquests.[3] Although the document exists incompletely today, it represents the clearest and most consistent teaching of Las Casas on the proper method of proclaiming the Gospel message. What exactly does Las Casas mean by "the one and only way"? What principles and teachings from the Bible does he employ to illustrate his arguments?

The Only Way of Attracting All Peoples to the True Religion
It is impossible for there to be any people, nation, or an entire society in whichever region, province, or rule, that could be so insensible and foolish to lack the capacity for [receiving] the teaching of the gospel. . . .

In sum, it must be admitted that our Indian nations not only have diverse expressions of natural intelligence . . . but that truly all of them exhibit innate ingenuity. Indeed, for the most part, one discovers amongst them more naturally skilled persons to govern human affairs than in other parts of the world. . . .

In the discussion that follows . . . we shall reflect on the way that is certainly natural, common, single and uniform by which all the elect and predestined shall be led to faith in Christ and the Christian religion. By means of that invitation, described just above, divine predestination is fulfilled. Our principal aim is to ponder this subject as needed before we complete this first book. Therefore, let us establish the following conclusion to illustrate this aim:

The one and only way of teaching all humanity the true religion was established by divine providence for the whole world and for all times—through rational persuasion of the intellect and the gentle attraction or incitement of the will. This way should be common to all peoples of the world, regardless of sects, errors, or corrupt customs.

This conclusion will be proven in various ways drawn from reasons; examples from the ancient Fathers; the teaching and form of preaching established by Christ for all times; the Apostles carrying out the practice entrusted to them; the authority of holy teachers; the traditional customs of the Church and its numerous laws.

And this conclusion is initially shown by means of reasons, of which here is the first: the one and only way proportionate to divine wisdom by which it disposes and moves all created things to their acts and ends proper to nature is gentle, attractive, and pleasant. But, among all created things, rational creatures are higher and more excellent than those which were not made to the image of God. . . . Therefore, divine wisdom moves rational creatures, that is, human beings, to their actions or works with gentleness, sweetness, and pleasantness. And according to the teaching of the faith, human beings are moved and led to the true religion only from the universal mandate, close to the end of Matthew's Gospel [28:19–20]: "Go teach all nations, baptizing them in the name of the Father, and of the Son, and of the Holy Spirit, teaching them to observe all that I have commanded you." And St. Paul's Letter to the Romans (10:17): "Faith comes from what is heard, and what is heard from the word of Christ." Therefore, the way of teaching human beings the true religion should be gentle, attractive, and pleasant. This way is through rational persuasion and the attraction of the will. . . .

Seeing that divine wisdom provides for the whole of creation, not only with respect to its natural actions or operations, but also by bestowing and impressing it with certain forms and powers, which are the principles of acts so that by themselves each thing may be inclined to these activities. Thus the activities whereby they are moved by God become connatural to creatures in a gentle and easy manner. For each thing has within itself some principle whose purpose is gently set by their natural inclination, just as a rock is directed by gravity by tending downwards naturally and gently.

And thusly, creatures move along and are led to their final ends as if tending spontaneously toward them. For this reason, it says in Wisdom (8:1) that divine wisdom "extends from end to end mightily," which is to say, it works for the perfection of all things. According to the biblical gloss, it gently disposes all things. Each thing, from the nature that has been divinely instilled in it, tends toward that which is established by divine wisdom, according to the need impressed upon the inclination. Since everything proceeds from God, insofar as it is good, which follows from Dionysius [Chapters 3 and 4 *On the Divine Names*] and Augustine [*City of God*, Book 21, Chapter 22]; therefore, all created things have received an imprint from God inclining them to desire the good, that is, their perfection. Hence the proper activity of each thing is its own end. . . . That which attains its own well-being through its proper activity is called virtuous and good, this end having been arranged by God, according to each thing's condition. . . .

First, it is evident because it is incomprehensible that God would make less provision for those who love the supernatural good than those creatures who desire a natural good. Therefore, to a much greater extent God moves and pours out to human beings who seek after the eternal good certain supernatural forms and qualities according to which He leads them toward the eternal good gently and promptly.

. . . Second, it is evident because the movement initiated through the teaching of the faith so that rational creatures are directed toward their proper acts or works, and seek after the supernatural eternal good, should be most similar to (and in no way contrary) to the movement that divine wisdom disposes and establishes in all created things. Otherwise, the divine arrangement and established order of things is denigrated; additionally, the dignity of the rational creature that God created with such esteem is denigrated. For it would appear that God indeed makes less provision for them than other inferior creatures, which have nevertheless been provided for the sake of the rational creature, and this would be most unsuitable. Therefore, whoever says or does anything to the contrary can be said to be a violator and destroyer of the divinely established order. But the movement and way by which divine wisdom moves all created things, and especially rational creatures, so that they may pursue their own good—natural or supernatural—is gentle, attractive, and pleasant. The way of rational creatures is conducive to divine wisdom to an even greater extent than other things and creatures.

Lastly, since the law of Christ is one and singular, never changing as to yesterday or until the end of time (and since there is only one faith and Christian religion), then there is only a single teaching of the faith established by Christ, preached to the apostles, received by the universal Church, and always proclaimed and observed. Finally, one and singular is the (human) species of the rational creature, which have themselves been individually scattered throughout the whole world. Of course, for them Christ has taught them the law, and the Catholic faith announced and proclaimed by the apostles and their followers, when he said: "Go into the whole world and proclaim the gospel to every creature" [Mark 16:15] and "Go teach all nations" [Matthew 28:19].

Document 13. "If they refuse to listen, we must go to other places": *In Defense of the Indians*, 1550–1552

This document expands Las Casas's life-long argument in favor of a peaceful method of evangelization rooted in the Bible.[4] It focuses specifically on the life and teachings of Jesus as the perfect model to follow in the context of what was happening in the Indies. Las Casas was directly opposed to the method endorsed by the Spanish imperial humanist, Juan Ginés de Sepúlveda, who supported the use of war and conquest to bring about the conversion of native Americans. Work through the four major arguments of Las Casas's position. Why does he think the Spaniards have no authority or jurisdiction over the Amerindian peoples? At one point, Las Casas mentions the example of Vera Paz (True Peace) from his missionary days in northern Guatemala during the 1530s in which he and several other Dominicans brought the Gospel peacefully to an otherwise unwelcoming and terrified indigenous community. Does the experience of Vera Paz provide a persuasive test case for Las Casas's arguments?

I readily grant that the Church is obliged to preach the gospel, as is said in the last chapters of Matthew and Mark: "Go out to the whole world; proclaim the Good News [gospel] to all creation"; "Go . . . make disciples of all nations, etc."; "It is a duty which has been laid on me. I should be punished if I did not preach it" [Mark 16:5; Matthew 28:19; 1 Corinthians 9:16]. These words are commands and indicate necessity. However, it does not follow from this that we can force unbelievers to hear the gospel. This is proved in four ways.

The first is that since unbelievers cannot be forced to receive the faith, with much less reason can they be forced to hear the words of the gospel, which are the way to faith. Indeed, if I cannot be forced to a religion, neither can I be forced to hear the dogmas and traditions of religion. Nor is it valid to say, "Faith comes by what is preached, and what is preached comes from the word of Christ" [Romans 10:17]. For just as unbelievers are not forced to religion when they cannot be forced to it without warfare, which brings all kinds of evil and results in hatred of our religion rather than an argument for the Catholic faith, so also we cannot force unbelievers who live in their own kingdoms to listen to the gospel, except by means of countless killings, arson, and destruction of their cities. Thus it would be sacrilegious and stupid to wage war on unbelievers in order that they may hear the gospel, because out of this would arise hatred of our religion instead of the advance of the faith.

The second argument is that since the Church is always vigilant and solicitous about conditions favorable to the Christian flock and never forces unbelievers who are its subjects in law and fact (for example, such subjects of Christian rulers as the Jews and Saracens) to hear the word of God, the conclusion is inseparable that unbelievers who are not subject either in law or in fact must not be forced to hear the word of God.

The third argument is the fact that Christ commanded only that the gospel be preached throughout the world. So wherever the gospel is preached, Christ's command is considered to have been carried out, and those who do not want to listen to the preachers bring guilt on themselves and will give an accounting to God. In this case, one can apply the advice of the wise man: "Where no one listens, do not pour out words" [Sirach 32:6].

The fourth argument is that it is quite clear from the instructions with which Christ first sent his disciples to preach the gospel what should be done when unbelievers do not want to hear the gospel. For we read:

> As you enter his house, salute it, and if the house deserves it, let your peace descend upon it; if it does not, let your peace come back to you. And if anyone does not welcome you or listen to what you have to say, as you walk out of the house or town shake the dust from your feet. I tell you solemnly, on the day of judgement, it will not go as hard with the land of Sodom and Gomorrah as with that town. (Matthew 10:12–15; Mark 6:10–11; Luke 9:4–5, 10:5–12)

Note that Christ did not teach that those who refuse to hear the gospel must be forced or punished. Rather, he will reserve their punishment to himself on the day of judgment, just as he also reserves the punishment of those who refuse to believe. . . .

Therefore, just as by punishing unbelievers who refuse to accept the gospel the Church would be usurping a right the Lord reserves for himself, so also would it be called a usurper if it forced unbelievers to listen to the gospel. For the reason is the same in each case, that is, that Christ has reserved the punishment to be inflicted for each offense to himself on the day of judgment. . . .

Note that Christ taught by word and deed that unbelievers must not be forced to hear the gospel. If they refuse to listen, we must go to other places, until we find friendly listeners. Now by the command of the Eternal Father we are obliged to hear, that is, to imitate Christ: "This is my beloved Son; he enjoys my favor. Listen to him" [Luke 9:54–56]. For he has been given as a "leader and master of the nations" [Isaiah 55:4]. Nor does it make any difference if someone replies that unbelievers will never become Christians if they cannot be forced to listen to the gospel. To this we say that we must not have more diligent concern for the salvation of men than Christ himself, who shed his precious blood for them: "It is enough for the disciple that he should grow to be like his teacher." "The fully trained disciple will always be like his teacher" [Matthew 10:25; Luke 6:40; John 13:13–16]. Let us imitate the examples and teachings of Christ and the Apostles and let his image shine forth in our conduct. Let us represent our teacher and savior by our deeds, and then those who have been foreordained to go from paganism to eternal life will hasten of their own free will to the sheepfold of Christ, to the city of God, to the place outside of which there is no salvation. If, however, we live like Christians and teach unbelievers in the way mentioned and they neglect to hear us or be converted, it is not our fault. Nor do I think there is any other reason why the Saracens, Turks, and other unbelievers refuse to embrace our faith than that we deny in practice what we affirm in our speech. It is not impossible, then, for unbelievers to embrace the faith just because it is unlawful to make an armed attack against them in order that they might listen to the gospel. The most effective solution is for them to see the Christian life shine in our conduct. But to advance the gospel by the power of arms is not Christian example but a pretext for stealing the property of others and subjugating their provinces.

The best solution for ending these seditious and diabolical crimes would be to send, from areas that have already been pacified and in which some have embraced our faith, representatives chosen from among the recent converts, in the name of some pious and religious men to whom they are devoted. These representatives would tell the other peoples in that province the purpose for which those pious men, who are vastly different in their conduct from the other, murderous men, come into those provinces, that is, to proclaim to them the way of truth and the worship of the true God. This is how we are destined to bring vast provinces to the faith. Afterward it would be useful to build a fortification in a suitable place where the preachers would have their residence a garrison of good and honest men had been installed. Now since these members of the garrison would not seek the death or the wealth of the Indians, the monarch would be obliged to give them an abundant salary.

In this gentle and Christian way, without tumult and the clash of arms, with only the word of Christ and the kindness of our soldiers, and with mildness and good services by which even wild beasts become tame, we have led to the faith some Tecultan provinces that are part of the kingdom of Guatemala. For we sent to them some of the recent converts who both loved and respected us. These men explained to the others that we came to them out of zeal for the house of God and to wake them from the ignorance by which they were bound for so many centuries, not to despoil them for their property and freedom as the other Spaniards were doing. All natural things want to be directed to their end gently. This is how we are moved by the Lord, who "orders all things to good" [Wisdom 8:1]. This great gift was granted to me and my companions by Christ, for we joined so many thousands of souls to their creator and savior by gentleness and kindness, without violence. Thus, they were happy that we lived among them, with the result that an area shortly before was filled with anger and pursued our men with a dangerous hatred because of the tremendous evils they had frequently inflicted upon it, put aside its fierceness; it was made more peaceful. The result is that, under the rule of our most invincible Prince Philip, son of the great Emperor Charles, they are called the provinces of True Peace [Vera Paz]. Nor do I doubt that by this work, which he condescended to accomplish through us, the weakest of all, Christ wanted to show the absurdity of the way in which the gospel had previously been preached to those peoples, how far from his teaching were the slaughter and arson committed by most wicked men against those pitiable peoples, and how his gospel was to be preached to them from that time on.

Now whoever, by preaching the gospel in this way, seeks to impose the sweet yoke of Christ on peoples gently, rather than violently, satisfies Christ's command, for he has followed his instruction and example. But whoever preaches the gospel in the other way, that is, with arms, have already strayed from Christ's teaching, nor in his sight can he be excused in any way. For evils must not be committed "as a means to good," nor should impiety be committed under the pretext of piety (Romans 3:8).

From the foregoing it is evident that war must not be waged against the Indians under the pretext that they should hear the preaching of Christ's teaching, even if they may have killed preachers, since they do not kill preachers as preachers or Christians as Christians, but as their most cruel public enemies, in order that they may not be oppressed or murdered by them. Therefore, let those who, under the pretext of spreading the faith, invade, steal, and keep their possessions of others by force of arms—let them fear God, who punishes perverse endeavors.

V
Apologist and Critic

In this section, Las Casas clearly emerges as an apologist (or defender) of the Amerindians, their cultural integrity, and their basic rights. He probed deeply into their religions, languages, government, social and economic relationships and into dozens of other areas to establish their clear identity as civilized peoples with all the rights and privileges of a free community organized into recognizable social polities. The famous letter of Pope Paul III (1534–1549) also stands out here for its significance in the history of Amerindian rights. Las Casas consistently defends the rationality of the natives against any Spanish prejudices toward non-European cultures. Inspired by the prophetic tradition of the Bible, Las Casas also had no qualms about indicting what he considered the dangerous elements of Aristotle's political thought, which had been deployed to justify the oppression of innocent peoples. The friar carried on this battle most notably in the debate at Valladolid with the reputed translator of Aristotle and imperial humanist Juan Ginés de Sepúlveda. Ultimately, Las Casas saw himself as fighting a larger spiritual battle in the name of truth and justice for the natives against the diabolical work of unjustifiable violence and oppression.

Document 14. "All humankind is one": *Apologetic History*, 1527–1561

As a Renaissance thinker, Las Casas looked at not only his religious tradition but also classical philosophy to affirm the unity of all peoples.[1] He turned to the Stoicism of the first-century BC Roman statesman Cicero, for example, to proclaim the common rationality and oneness of humankind. This provided Las Casas with a principle of fundamental human equality.[2] According to this elevated view of humanity, all peoples have the capacity to learn new things and grow in virtue and wisdom. Since everyone is made in the image of God, all peoples possess intelligence and free choice. What evidence does Las Casas employ to demonstrate the unity and equality of all peoples? Does a lack of political development among certain peoples imply the absence of natural reason and order? In what sense are his arguments "modern" or not?

There have never been peoples in the world, however rude, uncivilized, wild and barbarous, uncouth, fierce and hostile or almost savage they may be, who cannot be persuaded and brought to a comprehensive good order and structure of life; and made docile, mild, and friendly using industry and art, which is appropriate and natural for the majority of humanity; namely, by means of love and gentleness, kindness and joy.

The reason for this truth, as Cicero puts it in Book 1 of *The Laws*, is that all peoples of the world are human beings, and with respect to all men and each and every man there is a single definition: that they are rational beings. Everyone possesses his own knowledge, will, and free choice as formed to the image and likeness of God. All men have five external senses and four interior ones and are moved by the same objects of those senses. Everyone has the natural principles and seeds to understand, to learn, to know truths and about things unknown. This not only applies to those well-disposed but is also found in those who are evil because of their vicious customs. Everyone rests in the good and takes pleasure in what is delightful and joyful; and everyone rejects and detests what is evil and avoids what is unpleasant and what causes them harm.

[According to Cicero:] Nor is there any member of any nation who cannot attain moral excellence by using nature as his guide. The similarity between human beings is evident in their vices as well as their virtues. They are all beguiled by pleasure, which, though it leads on to vice, bears some resemblance to what is naturally good; for it gives delight by its lightness and charm. . . . What community does not love friendliness, generosity, and an appreciative mind that remembers acts of kindness? What community does not reject the arrogant, the wicked, the cruel, and the ungrateful—yes, and hate them too? So, since the whole human race is seen to be knit together, the conclusion is that the principles of right living make everyone a better person.[3]

Thus, all humankind is one and all men are alike with respect to their origin and the things of nature. No one is born educated. Therefore, all of us have need from the beginning to be guided and helped by others born before us. So, when some rustic peoples are discovered in the world, they are like uncultivated land, which easily produces bad weeds and useless thorns, yet contains within itself the seeds of natural virtue that when it is tilled and cultivated it brings forth agreeable, healthy, and abundant fruit.

All the nations of the world have understanding and will, and that which proceeds from these two powers in man is called free choice. And consequently, everyone has the power, aptitude, or capacity and by good natural inclination to be taught, persuaded, and drawn to order and reason, law and virtue, and to every goodness.

It logically follows that it is utterly impossible for there to exist a nation in which everyone is incapable, and thus so barbaric and lacking such reason, of being governed. There is no nation that cannot be persuaded, attracted, and taught whatever good moral doctrine, or instructed in matters of faith, or capable of receiving the Christian religion. . . . And this applies even to the case of the peoples of these lands who are found living desolate and separated, rather than in communities under the life of the city. It also refers to others who do not live in communities either small or large, but rather as nomads or vagrants, living without order like the wild. Of the latter a few have been discovered on the coast of the mainland in a place we call Florida. . . . Nevertheless, they are still rational persons and capable of order and reason. Rather, it is that they have not yet cultivated as a people and are living in a primitive state just like every other nation did before someone came to instruct them.

Document 15. "Those Indians . . . should not be deprived of freedom": *Sublimis Deus*, Pope Paul III, 1537

In 1537, Pope Paul III met in Rome with the Dominican Bernardino de Minaya, who related the treatment of the peoples of the New World at the hands of Spaniards.[4] The pope then wrote three letters to address these abuses, the third of which was *Sublimis Deus*. These landmark letters have even been called "the first intercontinental proclamation of inherent rights for all persons and the freedom of nations."[5] Las Casas referred to *Sublimis Deus* throughout his writings as the "new" *decretal* (or papal letter), implying that it had replaced certain letters of earlier popes explicitly and tacitly supporting Iberian conquest as a tool for spreading Christianity. What notable principles does the pope articulate in *Sublimis Deus*? Which teachings of Las Casas appear operative in the papal letter?

Paul, bishop, servant of the servants of God, to all of Christ's faithful who shall consider this letter, greetings and the apostolic blessing:

The sublime God so loved humanity that He made us not only so that we share in the good of existence like other creatures, but also so that we are able to reach the unattainable and invisible Highest Good and see Him face to face. According to the testimony of Sacred Scripture, we were created for eternal life and happiness, which no one finally attains except through faith in our Lord Jesus Christ. It is necessary to confess that man is of such a condition and nature that he can receive the faith of Christ, and whosoever possesses human nature, is himself capable of receiving the faith. Neither is it credible that anyone can be so inept as to want to obtain the end of what he believes and be denied the most essential means of attaining it.

Hence Truth Himself, who neither deceives nor can be deceived, entrusted the apostles of the faith with the duty of preaching, and said to them (Matthew 28:19): "Go teach all the nations." He meant this for all peoples, without any distinction, since every human being can learn the faith. The enemy of the human race (Satan), who opposes all good things to bring about ruin, seeing and envying this, devised a method hitherto unheard of, by which to prevent the word of God from being preached to peoples for the sake of salvation. The enemy provoked certain accomplices of his whom, desiring to satisfy his greed, dare to assert that the Indians of the West and South (and other peoples who have come to our attention in these times) should be reduced to our services like brute animals, under the pretext that they are wanting of the Catholic faith. They reduce the Indians to slavery, oppressing them with so many torments that brute animals placed in bondage are scarcely treated as such.

Therefore, we, although unworthy, bear the vicariate of our same Lord over the earth, and with every effort seek to lead the sheep of the flock entrusted to us, who are outside His sheepfold, toward it. Regarding the Indians, themselves being truly human, not only are they capable of embracing the Christian faith, but (as has been made known to us) hasten to it most willingly. Also, desiring to supply suitable remedies for these evil things, we declare the following:

Those Indians (and all other peoples who will be discovered by Christians in the future), although they are outside the faith, should not be deprived of their freedom and their ownership of things. Indeed, they can use, control, and enjoy their liberty and ownership freely and lawfully. Nor should they be reduced to slavery. If the contrary were to happen, it would be void and useless, having neither force nor influence. By virtue of apostolic authority, we declare that those same Indians and other peoples should be attracted to the proper faith of Christ by the preaching of God's word and by good example.

We decree that the copies of the present letters, underwritten in hand by a public notary, having secured with him by seal of some appointed ecclesiastical dignitary, should be given the same confidence used with the original (notwithstanding whatever previous letter and other contrary requests).

Given in Rome at the place of St. Peter, of the year Fifteen Hundred and Thirty-Seven, on June 2 of the third year of our pontificate.

Document 16. "Good-bye, Aristotle!": *In Defense of the Indians*, 1550–1552

The strategic use of Aristotle's political ideas to justify conquest and enslavement of "barbarians" in the New World was common among the learned elites.[6] John Major, a Scottish theologian teaching in Paris, was the first to apply Aristotle in this way. Like Major and Bishop Quevedo, the Spanish humanist Sepúlveda also appealed to Aristotle's doctrine on natural slavery as one of the convenient political devices for imperialism. These European thinkers viewed the Indians as brutes and irrational people incapable of governing themselves. Las Casas was opposed to this ancient political doctrine, often applied to deny the rational integrity and value present in foreign cultures. Which path does Las Casas promote as an alternative to Aristotle? What implications does belief in cultural imperialism have for modern race doctrines?

Rational nature, after the angelic, is nobler and more perfect than all other created things, and thus is the best and noblest part of the whole universe, to the extent that it has a greater resemblance to God. Thus, if the majority of men were freaks, even in their bodies—for example, having their eyes in their foreheads or being deaf-mutes, the conclusion would be that the perfection of the universe (which, as we have said above, is God's principal intention in the act of creation) would lack something in one of its nobler parts. It would, in the majority of cases, be suffering evil or a mistake of nature or abnormalities, something does not occur in other creatures. Thus, the plan of God, who wills the universe to be as beautiful and perfect as possible, would be in great part frustrated. But this is entirely unfitting and quite false. Therefore, it is impossible that dullness in natural power and in the higher faculties, as well as in the internal senses that serve the higher faculties for understanding well, will be found in the majority of men. Rather, we find that for the most part men are intelligent, far sighted, diligent, and talented, so that it is impossible for a whole region or country to be slow-witted and stupid, moronic, or suffering from similar natural defects or abnormalities. We have discussed this more fully in our treatise *The Only Way of Attracting All Peoples to the True Religion*, where we made this conclusion evident by arguments and citations; that is, that it would be impossible to find one whole race, nation, region, or country anywhere in the world that is slow-witted, moronic, foolish, or stupid, or even not having for the most part sufficient natural knowledge and ability to rule and govern itself.

To those who are barbarians in this absolute, strict, and proper sense we should apply what the Philosopher says in the *Politics*, that they ought to be governed by the Greeks, that is, by those who are wiser, for nature makes them slaves because of the dullness and brutality of their disposition. Since they are far removed from what is best in human nature, they ought to be ruled by others so that they can be taught how to live in a civilized and human way. In turn, because they are generally strong, they should perform services for their masters. Thus, both master and slave benefit.

The Philosopher adds that it is lawful to catch or hunt barbarians of this type like wild beasts so that they might be led to the right way of life. Two points must be noted here. First, to force barbarians to live in a civilized and human way is not lawful for anyone and everyone, but only for monarchs and rulers of states. Second, it must be borne in mind that barbarians must not be compelled harshly in the manner described by the Philosopher but are to be gently persuaded and lovingly drawn to accept the best way of life. For we are commanded by divine law to love our neighbor as ourselves, and since we want our own vices to be corrected and uprooted gently, we should do the same to our brothers, even if they are barbarians. This is what we are taught by Paul: "We who are strong have a duty to put up with the qualms of the weak without thinking of ourselves.

Each of us should think of his neighbors and help them to become stronger Christians. Christ did not think of himself." And, a little further along: "It can only be to God's glory, then, for you to treat each other in the same friendly way as Christ treated you" [Romans 15:1–2, 7].

Again, if we want to be sons of Christ and followers of the truth of the gospel, we should consider that, even though these peoples may be completely barbaric, they are nevertheless created in God's image. They are not forsaken by divine providence that they are incapable of attaining Christ's kingdom. They are our brothers, redeemed by Christ's most precious blood, no less than the wisest and most learned men in the whole world. Finally, we must consider it possible that some of them are predestined to become renowned and glorious in Christ's kingdom. Consequently, to these men who are wild and ignorant in their barbarism we owe the right which is theirs, that is, brotherly kindness and Christian love, according to Paul: "I owe a duty to Greeks just as much as to barbarians, to the educated just much as to the uneducated, and it is this that makes me want to bring the Good News to you too in Rome" [Romans 1:14–15]. Christ wanted love to be called his single commandment. This we owe to all men. Nobody is exempted. "There is no room for distinction between Greek and Jew, between the circumcised and the uncircumcised, or between barbarian and Scythian, slave and free man. There is only Christ: he is everything and is in everything" [Colossians 3:17].

Therefore, although the Philosopher, who was ignorant of Christian truth and love, writes that the wise may hunt down barbarians in the same way as they would wild animals, let no one conclude from this that the barbarians are to be killed or loaded like beasts of burden with excessive, cruel, hard, and harsh labor and that, for this purpose, they can be hunted and captured by wiser men. Goodbye, Aristotle! From Christ, the eternal truth, we have the command "You must love your neighbor as yourself" [Matthew 22:40]. And again Paul says, "Love is not selfish" [1 Corinthians 13:5] but seeks the things of Jesus Christ. Christ seeks souls, not property. He who alone is the immortal king of kings thirsts not for riches, not for ease and pleasures, but for the salvation of mankind, for which, fastened to the wood of the cross, he offered his life. He who wants a large part of mankind to be such that, following Aristotle's teachings, he may act like a ferocious executioner toward them, press them into slavery, and through them grow rich, is a despotic master, not a Christian; a son of Satan, not God; a plunderer, not a shepherd; a person who is led by the spirit of the devil, not heaven. If you seek Indians so that gently, mildly, quietly, humanely, and in a Christian manner you may instruct them in the word of God and by your labor bring them to Christ's flock, imprinting the gentle Christ on their minds, you perform the work of an apostle and will receive an imperishable crown of glory from our sacrificed lamb. But if it be in order that by sword, fire, massacre, trickery, violence, tyranny, cruelty, and an inhumanity that is worse than barbaric you may destroy and plunder utterly harmless peoples who are ready to renounce evil and receive the word of God, you are children of the devil and the most horrible plunderers of all. "My yoke," says Christ, "is easy and my burden light" [Matthew 11:30]. You impose intolerable burdens and destroy the creatures of God, you who ought to be life to the blind and light to the ignorant.

Document 17. "Every nation . . . has the right to defend itself": *In Defense of the Indians*, 1550–1552

In this document[7] from the *Apologia*, Las Casas continues his discussion of the "barbarian" as a political tool for European expansion. How does Las Casas define the category of the "barbarian" in a manner different from Aristotle and Sepúlveda? Las Casas also raises serious doubts about the credibility of history told from the perspective of those in power. He refers to the Spanish chronicler Gonzalo Fernández de Oviedo (d. 1557). In addition to being one of the first Spaniards who read the Requirement to natives, Oviedo's official historical account of the Indies supplied imperial humanists like Sepúlveda with ammunition to justify conquest of the Amerindians for their alleged depravity and barbarism. What makes Las Casas's arguments in this reading so radical and controversial for his time and for our global conflicts today?

Because of the points we have proved and made clear, the distinction the Philosopher [Aristotle] makes between the two above-mentioned kinds of barbarian is evident. For those he deals with in the first book of the *Politics*, and whom we have just discussed, are barbarians without qualification, in the proper and strict sense of the word, that is, dull-witted and lacking in the reasoning powers necessary for self-government. They are without laws, without king, etc. For this reason they are by nature unfitted for rule.

However, he admits, and proves, that the barbarians he deals with in the third book of the same work some have a lawful, just, and natural government. Even though they lack the art of use of writing, they are not wanting in the capacity and skill to rule and govern themselves, both publicly and privately. Thus they have kingdoms, communities, and cities that they govern wisely according to their laws and customs. Thus their government is legitimate and natural, even though it has some resemblance to tyranny. From these statements we have no choice but to conclude that the rulers of such nations enjoy the use of reason and that their people and the inhabitants of their provinces do not lack peace and justice. Otherwise they could not be established or preserved as political entities for long. . . .

Now if we shall have shown that among our Indians of the western and southern shores (granting that we call them barbarians and they are barbarians) there are important kingdoms, large numbers of people who live settled lives in a society, great cities, kings, judges and laws, persons who engage in commerce, buying, selling, lending, and the other contracts of the law of nations, will it not stand proved that the Reverend Doctor Sepúlveda has spoken wrongly and viciously against people like these, either out of malice or ignorance of Aristotle's teaching, and, therefore, has falsely and perhaps irreparably slandered them before the entire world? From the fact that the Indians are barbarians it does not necessarily follow that they are incapable of government and must be ruled by others, except to be taught about the Catholic faith and to be admitted to the holy sacraments. They are not ignorant, inhuman, or bestial. Rather, long before they had heard the word Spaniard they had properly organized states, wisely ordered by excellent laws, religion, and custom. They cultivated friendship and, bound together in common fellowship, lived in populous cities in which they wisely administered the affairs of both peace and war justly and equitably, truly governed by laws that at very many points surpass ours, and could have won even the admirations of the sages of Athens.

Now if Sepúlveda had wanted, as a serious man should, to know the full truth before he sat down to write with his mind corrupted by the lies of tyrants, he should have consulted the honest religious who have lived among those peoples for many years and know their endowments of character and industry, as well as the progress they have made in religion and morality. . . .

This is what you, a man of such great scholarship, should have done in ascertaining the truth, instead of writing, with the sharp edge of your pen poised for the whispers of irresponsible men, your little book that slanders the Indian inhabitants of such a large part of the earth. Do you quote to us Oviedo's *History*, which bears the approval of the Royal Council, as though Oviedo, as he himself testifies (Book 6, chap. 8), was not a despotic master who kept unfortunate Indians oppressed by slavery like cattle and, in imitation of the other thieves, ruined a great part of the continent, as though the Council, when it approves a book, appears to approve also all the lies it contains, or as if, when the Council approves a book, it knows whether its contents are true? To this enemy you give your belief, as also to the one who is an interested party. For he possessed an allotment of Indians, as did the other tyrannical masters.

From this it is clear that the basis for Sepúlveda's teaching that these people are uncivilized and ignorant is worse than false. Yet even if we were to grant that this race has no keenness of mind or artistic ability, certainly they are not, in consequence, obliged to submit themselves to those who are more intelligent and to adopt their ways, so that, if they refuse, they may be subdued by having war waged against them and be enslaved, as happens today. For men are obliged by the natural law to do many things they cannot be forced to do against their will. We are bound by the natural law to embrace virtue and imitate the uprightness of good men. No one, however, is punished for being bad unless he is guilty of rebellion. Where the Catholic faith has been preached in a Christian manner and as it ought to be, all men are bound by natural law to accept it, yet no one is forced to accept the faith of Christ. No one is punished because he is sunk in vice, unless he is rebellious or harms the property or persons of others. No one is forced to embrace virtue and show himself as a good man. One who receives a favor is bound by the natural law to return the favor by what we call antidotal obligation. Yet no one is forced to this, nor is he punished if he omits it, according to the common interpretation of the jurists.

To relieve the need of a brother is a work of mercy to which nature inclines and obliges men, yet no one is forced to give alms. . . . Therefore, not even a truly wise man may force an ignorant barbarian to submit to him, especially by yielding his liberty, without doing him an injustice. This the poor Indians suffer, with extreme injustice, against all the laws of God and of men and against the law of nature itself. For evil must not be done that good may come of it. . . .

Now if, on the basis of this utterly absurd argument, war against the Indians were lawful, one nation might rise up against another and one man against another man, and on the pretext of superior wisdom, might strive to bring the other into subjection. On this basis the Turks, and the Moors—the truly barbaric scum of the nations—with complete right and in accord with the law of nature could carry on war, which, as it seems to some, is permitted to us by a lawful decree of the state. If we admit this, will not everything high and low, divine and human, be thrown into confusion? What can be proposed more contrary to the eternal law than what Sepúlveda often declares? What plague deserves to be more loathed? I am of the opinion that Sepúlveda, in his modesty, thinks Spain regards other nations as wiser than herself. Therefore, she must be forced to submit to them according the eternal law! And, indeed, the eternal law has arranged and determined all things in admirable proportion and order. It separated kingdom from kingdom and people from people "when the Most High gave the nations their inheritance, when he divided the sons of men" [Deuteronomy 32:8]. Also, each nation placed over itself, under divine guidance, a king and rulers: "Over each nation he has set a governor" [Sirach 17:14]. For all kings and rulers, even among the barbarians, are servants of God, as divine wisdom teaches: "By me monarchs rule and princes issue just laws; by me rulers govern and the great impose justice on the world" [Proverbs 8:15–16]. And all the kings and governors who fail to rule their subjects rightly, barbarians or not, believers or not, are violators of the eternal law and face God, who is the avenging judge of that transgression. Since, therefore, every nation by the eternal law has a ruler or prince, it is wrong for one nation to attack another under the pretext of being superior in wisdom or to overthrow other kingdoms. For it acts contrary to the eternal law, as we read in Proverbs [22:28]: "Do not displace the ancient landmark set up by your ancestors." This is not an act of wisdom, but of great injustice and a lying excuse for plundering others. Hence every nation, no matter how barbaric, has the right to defend itself against a more civilized one that wants to conquer it and take away its freedom. And, moreover, it can lawfully punish with death the more civilized as a savage and cruel aggressor against the law of nature. And this war is certainly more just than the one that, under pretext of wisdom, is waged against them.

VI

Political Philosopher

Las Casas in this section goes beyond that of mere apologist and critic and emerges as a sophisticated political philosopher in his own right. The previous section outlined how Las Casas fundamentally challenged the ancient political idea of natural slavery by supporting a native right of self-defense against imperial powers. However, we now see Las Casas strategically appealing to Aristotle to elaborate his own political philosophy and doctrine of rights though one grounded in his religious and humanitarian commitments toward reason, freedom and equality. Subjective rights—the language of modern human rights—were a confluence of ideas for him derived from ancient philosophy, Roman law, canon law, and the Bible. They were ideas tested and refined through his personal and pastoral experience working with indigenous peoples. Las Casas provided a comprehensive account of justice and rights protecting human freedom in political, economic, and religious matters, all of which can be seen in the following documents. The documents also include his views on war and on principles for determining when it was just for Christians and non-Christians to wage war.

Document 18. "Liberty is an innate right of all human beings": *On Royal Power*, ca. 1560s

This document[1] presents a portion of *De regia potestate* (*On Royal Power*), a strictly political treatise of Las Casas published in 1571 several years after his death. Most striking and modern is his claim that the people are the efficient and final cause of all royal power. The people freely choose a political authority whose purpose is not to create the law but to administer it with justice. However, in contrast to certain modern political theorists, Las Casas claims that the people do not give up some of their basic freedom and rights after appointing a ruler. What is the purpose of royal power and its limits according to this document? In what way is Aristotle now useful for Las Casas's political theory in contrast to Sepúlveda? How do the conceptions of civil authority and the common good here contrast with our current views about politics and the responsibility of political leaders?

First Principle

I.1. From the beginning of humanity, all human beings, all lands and all things, were free and unclaimed. According to natural right and the primordial law of nations, all were free, not subject to slavery. Certainly, with respect to human beings, it is shown that they are originally born free because of their rational nature [*Digest* 1.1.4]. Because of the equality of nature, God did not make anyone the slave of another, but gave a free will to everyone. The reason for this, according to St. Thomas Aquinas, is because "the rational nature is absolutely not ordained to another, as to its end; so too a man cannot be ordained to another man as his end" [II Sent. Dist. 44, q.1, a.3]. For liberty is an innate right of all human beings, according to necessity and for its own sake, which began with rational nature and from the law of nature [Gratian D.1, c.7]. . . .

I.4. The free man possesses freedom over himself [Aristotle, *Metaphysics* 1]—one who has the power to act freely, as he wishes, with respect to himself and using his possessions.

II.1. Inanimate things, such as land, goods, and the like, were also originally free according to natural right.

II.2. Likewise, slavery and servitude can in no way be presupposed, unless shown otherwise.

II.3. Those goods are called free and unclaimed, which are not recognized by anyone other than God. Everything that God has created has been given to those peoples under heaven [Deuteronomy 4:19]. By divine gift, each man has the power to take possession of anything, since everything was possessed in common from the beginning. Therefore, everything is unclaimed, lest it be proven otherwise [*Digest* 1.5.4].

II.5. But truly, liberty is an inviolable power.

III.1. According to the doctors, no kings and no emperor has the requisite authority over the goods of each individual person and the possessions of those goods; nor do they have it over the provinces and territories situated amongst them. They do not have ownership of use (*dominium utile*) nor direct control (*dominium directo*) of those possessions. Rather, the possessors of those goods are not referred to as vassals of kings and rulers but are subjects in the territories of kings and rulers with respect to jurisdiction.

III.8. Kings and emperors, and any other supreme rulers, have no direct control, not even usage of the private things of their inferiors, but are protectors and defenders with supreme jurisdiction.

Second Principle

IV.1. No subjugation, no servitude, and no manner of burden was ever legitimately imposed unless the people gave their voluntary consent to that imposed burden they were under.

This is proven in that, initially, all things and all peoples were free. If anything was done against the will of the people or the private ownership of a thing, it was force due to some doubt thus prohibiting the people from the use of their freedom, which pertains to the natural law. There is nothing more inconsistent with natural justice than to take away something against the will of an owner who does not wish to relinquish what is his own or be placed under the rule of another in some unlawful manner. Moreover, originally, all authority, power, and jurisdiction of kings and rulers came from a free people itself; and besides, any supreme magistrate who has imposed whatever census or tribute has done so from the free will of the people.

IV.2. However, civil (or legal) rights began when cities were founded and magistrates were established. [*Institutes* 2.1] The Roman people have transferred all power to the ruler as long as the burden remains.

IV.3. Whence rule (*imperium*) proceeded immediately from the people, and the community has been the efficient cause of kings, rulers, or any such magistrate, if they have been legitimately installed. Therefore, if the community has been the effective or efficient and final cause of kings and rulers, given that they have been established by the people through a free election, then rulers from the beginning would have not been able to impose on the people save the tributes and services which the people itself deemed agreeable.

IV.4. It follows that the community, upon electing a ruler or king, shall not lose its freedom, nor shall it entrust or concede the power to become oppressed, or exposed to violence, or that this thing or the other shall be done to the detriment of the whole people or community.

It would not have been necessary to explain this at the time when they were electing the king, because that which already belongs to it, even if it is not explicitly stated or declared, shall neither be altered nor increased. It is for this reason that the people may not be burdened, nor their freedom diminished, nor the whole community exposed to violence, without the necessary consent of the people intervening.

Another proof is that before there existed kings and magistrates, all the goods previously mentioned belonged to the whole community, and that this belonged to it according to natural right. The people, with respect to nature and time, are anterior to kings themselves. But the people had to present some of the public goods of which to maintain the king. Therefore, as noted, it was the people who made and constituted the rights of the king.

Third Principle

V.1. The power and jurisdiction of kings exists only to the extent that it procures the common good of the people; and this power and jurisdiction entails no interference with liberty, nor any detriment to it.

Fourth Principle

VI.1. If the king or ruler happens to have many kingdoms or cities, and one of which suffers the travails of war or faces other grave conditions, then other kingdoms and cities should, out of charity and natural duty, come to the aid of the one in need. Nevertheless, this must be done without serious damage to itself and provided that its own needs are met first. The assistance should be conducted voluntarily and not to avoid some evil or harm. Nor is it obligated by any law to expose itself to such danger verging on total annihilation or serious damage for the sake of promoting the good and welfare of another city.

The reason is . . . every city is a perfect community, and self-sufficient, whose very essence of life is the republic itself, according to Aristotle [1 *Politics*, 1252b28–1253a1]. Therefore, it must before all else look after its own defense and well-being. Consequently, it does not have the duty, to avoid some evil or harm, to promote the good and welfare of the kingdom or another part of the kingdom if it means exposing itself to extreme danger.

VI.2. This principle and rationale are proven because citizens by nature come from their own place of birth, their homeland (*patriae*).

So, they are obligated to fight in its defense and, for this reason, the city has power over its citizens. Therefore, if the citizens come from their homeland, then the *patriae* must be looked after first and foremost . . . whereby we must first quench our own thirst first with water and not another. And each one should first give care to himself before his neighbor.

First Conclusion

VIII.1. No ruler, no king, no matter how sovereign, can establish and declare anything within their jurisdiction, concerning the whole commonwealth, which is either injurious or to the detriment of the people and the subjects without their official and legal consent. If done otherwise, then there is no force of law.

The first part of the conclusion is provided based on authority and reason. For reason demonstrates the following: the people have been the efficient and final cause of kings and rulers, for which they have been ordained for the people, and for the good of the community, and the common welfare as to an end. Therefore, no kings can establish, ordain, or abolish anything that is harmful to the people and contrary to the welfare of their subjects.

Consequently, if something is ordained to another, the natural order does not appoint an impediment to it, so that something evil results, but rather for its assistance. The reason being that something which is ordained to another, as to an end, is the mean proportionate to its end. For the mean is only for the execution of the end. Now the people have taken up the means of electing and establishing kings, rulers, and leaders over themselves, to bring about their own end, which is to say, success, welfare, protection, and preservation of the common good (*boni communis*). Therefore, the community is the cause of itself. [Aristotle, 1 *Metaphysics*, 982b26–27] According to the order of nature, which must always be respected, it follows that the king or the ruler may not and cannot bring about the common good by some evil, but only by aiding. Therefore, no ruler, no king, no matter how sovereign, can establish and declare anything within their jurisdiction, which is to the detriment of the people and the subjects.

VIII.2. Second, everything that will have attained the end of government, such as the many affairs and activities, by necessity, is the norm taken from the supreme end, which disposes each thing in the best manner that is suitable for leading it to its own end. But the end of each and every free people is its good, indeed the welfare (*utilitas*) itself, which consists in those who are governed and the whole community being directed in their conduct to what is most beneficial, so that their defects may be supplied; the correction of their customs so they become virtuous; life in peace; increase and defense from enemies, not only externally but also from within. Therefore, the king or ruler shall not lawfully establish anything contrary to the righting of defects. . . .

VIII.4. Thirdly, no one without legitimate cause can inflict harm against the freedom of their people. If somebody establishes something contrary to the common welfare of the people without their consent, then it is a threat to the freedom of the people and the subjects.

VIII.5. Freedom is the most precious and inestimable of all goods that a free people can have [*Digest* 50.17.106]. Therefore, by threatening liberty, the ruler would act contrary to justice.

IX.1. Likewise, the ruler, king, or prince, of any kingdom or community, however great his sovereignty, does not have the freedom and power of ruling citizens as he wishes and according to what pleases his own will. He must only rule according to the laws of the state; whereas the laws must be fashioned to promote the welfare of the whole community and not its detriment. More importantly, the laws shall be made in service to the commonwealth and the good of the people, rather than the commonwealth for the laws. Hence the ruler has no power of decreeing anything injurious to the republic.

IX.2. The king or ruler, as a man, does not rule with subjugation, but is rather like a minister of the law (*minister legis*). He is therefore not a ruling master but administers the people through laws.

IX.3. For this reason they are called kings, who protect the laws under God, ordering what is just and prohibiting what is unjust. Thus, the citizens remain free, and do not submit to men as servants, but obey the laws.

No one has the power to act contrary to the laws of which there is no power to dispense. Otherwise, he would have exceeded the limits of his own power and whatever he did would have no force. It is indispensable for a ruler to do anything that preserves the common good. . . .

IX.4. No sovereign can do the impossible, which is contrary to the necessities of life. Necessity is from divine law and natural law, which the prince is unable to falsify, plunder, and corrupt. But if kings were to establish anything to the detriment of the people or their subjects, without the requisite consent of the latter, they do something prohibited by natural and divine law, which greatly displeases God. They themselves try to bring about what is not permissible. Therefore, they may not lawfully do what is harmful to the people. According to natural law one is prohibited from doing to another that which he would reasonably not want done to himself.

IX.5. Whatever a ruler does to the detriment of the whole kingdom contrary to their consent and will is against the natural order instilled by God in all things. And that ruler does what is contrary to natural right. This is proven because the ruler who has inflicted force and fear on his subjects causes involuntariness. Lack of consent is against the natural inclination of the will, which is itself free by nature, and may not be coerced.

Document 19. "Infidels rightly have ownership of their goods": *Certain Principles*, 1552

This document[2] concerning "certain principles" (*Principia quaedam*) for organizing social and political life belongs to a group of Las Casas's 1552 treatises published in Seville. Las Casas weaves together the Bible, scholastic theology, ancient philosophy, and civil and canon law to establish essential principles for good governance among both believers and nonbelievers. Only two of the four principles—on the ownership of property and political jurisdiction—are considered here. What is the political significance of the Bible for Las Casas? What is the "law of nations," and are there analogous or comparable concepts for organizing contemporary world politics?

First Principle

The ownership of things (*dominium rerum*) inferior to man applies to all human beings in the world with no exclusion of believers or unbelievers. This is in accord with divine justice and divine providence in what is common; and, certainly, natural right and the law of nations in what is particular.

First, this principle of divine justice and divine order is announced in Genesis (1:26): "Let us make man to our image and likeness and let him have dominion over the fishes of the sea, and the fowls of the air, and the beasts, and the whole earth." And further on: "Fill the earth and subdue it, and rule over the fishes of the sea," etc. These words demonstrate how God conceded to human nature the power signified by them, saying: "Let the earth bring forth the green herb," and with these words God gave the power of making trees. God said to human beings: "Rule over the fishes of the sea," etc. And similarly, with these words God gave to human beings power over created things and made them owners of things with respect to use and control. . . .

Second, it is also shown from natural right because God first created all things and gave to each thing and ordained it according to the purpose of its nature and condition. It is said that what pertains to each of them is of the law and natural right, which is from divine providence. In other words, it is given by the natural order having arranged each and every kind of thing, so that the matter and the form are constituted on account of the essence itself aiming toward perfection. For example, that humankind has hands and that the animals might serve man. And this refers to his preservation, such as health and the like. Whence each and every created thing is naturally owed that which is oriented toward its perfection and according to the order of divine providence.

Therefore, it is from justice that each and everything has its due and it is said that what is each one's own is that which is oriented toward the existence of the thing itself. It is from divine providence and natural law that all inferior things are arranged for man's use. The consequence is that man has natural mastery over those things that he must obtain and must have, and it is according to divine justice that man must possess what is necessary. . . .

The third point is that the ownership of inferior things applies to man with respect to the law, or right, of nations (*iure gentium*). That is because all created things have been given in common to all human beings by divine goodness and by divine providence. This was so from the beginning of the first human being given the power and the freedom to take and use those things. Any person had the power to take possession of each and every thing which from the beginning was in common to make it their own solely by seizing it. Moreover, his own act of taking possession of a thing from divine concession has made him into its owner. If he were alone, then he would have taken the thing for his own pleasure. If he were already living in a society with others, then it would come from a common agreement or pact seeing that such things have been particularly apportioned thereafter. Whence it follows that the common agreement or pact of the whole community and multitude, which is in accordance with the law of nations derived from natural reason, has introduced and approved that lands and material goods should be divided and apportioned. This is so that each person can take care of what is his own thing for the sake of preserving peace among men dwelling together and attaining other benefits as indicated by the experts.

The result thereupon was that each person was made a direct and particular owner of his things which were originally held in common and when there was no property he had yet taken. He became an owner as a result of divine providence and according to natural law, and also from the common agreement, considered pleasing at the approval of many who were dwelling together at that time so that later they could live together in harmony. Truly, the act of justice accomplishes something owed to another, which proceeds from giving to each what is his own. Whatever man has become an owner of material things, he has been sanctioned from justice and divine providence, natural law and the law of nations. For that reason, it pertains to human justice to inviolably preserve for whatever man his ownership of things—after all, justice is to give to each what is his own.

From this principle it follows first that "infidels rightly have ownership of their goods." This is shown because God made other creatures inferior to man indifferently on behalf of all rational creatures and in service to the many nations, as clear from what was stated, without any distinction among believers and unbelievers. Therefore, neither should we distinguish.

Second, it not lawful in any sense for whatever private or public person, without legitimate cause, to take away something that belongs to another against his will (whether a believer or unbeliever) after one becomes the owner. For it is unlawful for anyone, even those using public authority, to act contrary to justice, by which each person is preserved in his own right (*in iure suo*); or to violate the divine order or natural right and the law of nations. Even if one had taken such a thing in secret having committed theft, that would still be opposed to justice, which renders to each and every person what is his own. The act of theft entails violently taking over another's property against the owner's will. If, in fact, the robbery is violently committed in plain sight, then a certain violence and coercion has been done by which, contrary to justice, someone has been deprived of what is his own (Aquinas, *Summa theologiae*, II-II, 66.5, 8).

Second Principle

The rule of one man over others, which entails the duty of advising and directing others, is called authority or jurisdiction. And this is from natural right and the law of nations.

This is proven because if something is natural for whomever, it requires that without which it would not have the power even to exist in nature. For nature does not fail to give what is necessary [Aristotle, *De Anima*, 3]. But man is a social animal by nature. This is shown from the fact that one man alone is incapable of attaining all that is necessary for human life. Therefore, he is unable to be preserved without some human society. Humans are naturally prone to assembling together of which there is someone who oversees and rules the whole society. Without being ruled and governed human society is unable to be maintained. This is proven because if many humans existed and each of them did what is suitable for himself, the diverse multitude would scatter apart unless there was someone that could take care of them by directing them toward the good of the whole. Similarly, the body of a man (or whatever animal) falls apart and dies when there is not some shared regulatory power directing the body to the common good of all the members. . . . In the universe, bodies are directed by a chief heavenly body, or a certain order of divine providence, and all remaining bodies by the rational creature. As Augustine says in *On the Trinity* (Book 3), in a single human body a soul rules the body, while the parts of the soul—the irascible and the concupiscible—are governed by reason. Similarly, among the parts of the body there is a single principle like the heart or the head that moves all the parts. In the whole multitude there is something naturally that governs.

Therefore, it is natural in any human society or diverse social life to have a leader who seeks and promotes the common good. Otherwise, a community would not be preserved but would disperse. According to Sirach 17:14, "He gave to each nation a ruler." Therefore, the rule of one man over others, insomuch as it entails the duty of taking counsel and directing, is from natural law. . . .

Seeing that human beings themselves were unable to live in community apart from a leader, it was from common consent or agreement at the beginning that the whole multitude chose someone or some people who would direct and govern all of them to primarily take care of the whole common good. And it is thus evident that the natural rule or authority (*dominium*) of a man over others was introduced by natural law and was perfected or confirmed yet again by the law of nations. This is shown from Justinian's *Digest* (1.1.5): "From this law (of nations), peoples were distinguished, kingdoms founded." This was how the Roman people in the beginning chose an emperor by conceding all their power to him, yet without losing their liberty to transfer their rule and jurisdiction. . . .

The jurisdiction and power of the kings over the people and multitude was properly from the people, from whom the kings held immediate power. . . . Only in this way, that is, by means of the original election of the people, was there established the lawful authority and jurisdiction of the kings over human beings in the whole world and in many nations. Otherwise the rule would be unjust and tyrannical. Beside this, it could be established or introduced because of a special mandate of God, as it happened among the Israelites. This is seen in 1 Kings 1 and 8 and in Deuteronomy 17, where additionally coinciding with the election and consent, or the approval of the entire people, was God's mandate and arrangement.[3]

From this second principle it follows: among infidels there are also governments and authorities over peoples caused by the duty of taking counsel.

This is shown because every human being, whether unbeliever or believer, is a rational and social animal. Consequently, society or the desire to live in society is natural for everyone. Therefore, having kings and leaders among believers and unbelievers is natural. It follows that natural right and the law of nations is common to all human beings and general to all. As noted in Gratian on *ius naturale* (Dist. 1, c. 7) where it says that "natural right is common to every nation." And it says in the chapter on *ius gentium* (Dist. 1, c. 9), "The law of nations is called the same because nearly all peoples make use of it." It is evident that among believers and unbelievers, there is no difference as far as natural right and the law of nations is concerned. They justly and naturally exhibit the rule of one man over others, authorities, leaders, kings, *caciques*, chieftains, and these are known or called so by another name, who direct and govern communities and the multitudes of men and take care of the common good. We say that a king is one entrusted by the entire society or the multitude with supreme authority in human affairs. . . .

Any king or leader of a multitude has as much jurisdiction as necessary for exercising royal or governmental power; nevertheless, it is a power that originally resided in the community itself, which it transferred (as stated before) to the kings and leaders.

Second, it follows that without legitimate cause it is unlawful for anyone, not even a public authority, in whatever sense, to remove or usurp or obstruct some ruler or judge (not subject to anyone above) of the rule and authority which he has and exercises over his subjects, whether a believer or unbeliever.

This is evident because it is unlawful, even for those using public authority, to do injustice or injury to anyone, even infidels. To commit an injury to such a ruler by removing or impeding his right, rule, or authority which he legitimately has over his subjects is to also commit injury against the ruler's subjects. That is because no one may transgress or do what is contrary to natural right and the law of nations through which the rights extend to a temporal ruler or ruler of this sort and his authority (as already shown). It concerns the subjects to have their own natural ruler from their own native land (*patria*) and people; and that their ruler is free and able to freely govern his subjects and to care for public well-being and affairs.

Document 20. "The same right": *On the Treasures of Peru*, 1563

During his final years, Las Casas composed *On the Treasures of Peru* (*De thesauris*). This work[4] reiterated what he and many of the Dominican advocates had claimed since the beginning of the conquest of the Indies—restitution and more was required of Spanish Christians for past evils if they wished to inherit eternal life. The proposal in *On the Treasures of Peru* was unyielding: full restoration of native Inca sovereignty. What is "the same right" between the natives of Peru and all other peoples that Las Casas identifies in this document? Does he successfully balance his universal commitments with a respect for religious diversity? What does Las Casas mean by the term "dignity" and how does he apply the idea of dignity to address the widespread injustice of theft? What are the strengths and weaknesses of his account?

It is well known that the hiding of treasures and other precious objects by kings and powerful men in their tombs was a lawful and customary fact among ancient peoples, believers and unbelievers. The reason that can be assigned to this power is such: there is evidently a natural inclination belonging to all human beings, as rational creatures, to render the honor due to human nature, before the rest of the other animals; one knows that man has this honor because the human body is buried. Seeing that among all the animals only man is a sacred and divine animal; therefore, only man is bestowed this honor. His corpse is buried so that it is not lacerated by birds and other animals whereas the rest of the carcasses of animals stay unburied. The Philosopher [Aristotle] in Book 1 of the *Rhetoric* puts the tomb among the various parts of honor. . . .

The measure of injustice increases or decreases according to the level of the person's dignity suffering injury.

In fact, this is evident in our case [of Peru] insofar as each can reasonably conclude it: those who have received injury—be they kings, the most powerful, the richest lords—and who have fashioned tombs so great because of their honor, praise, and glory, offering most of their wealth to the dead. So, it is clear from what was said that the extent of injuries done in such things, which they have suffered from us, is of no small amount but numbers in the hundreds of thousands and millions. Such estimation is without comparison or measure among them and even in the writings of philosophers and wise persons in this world. It therefore remains that the great [injuries committed] by thieves of this sort must go beyond the restitution of treasures stolen, and make satisfaction—for this is the way of salvation.

If, however, such injuries are a matter treated in the court of conscience, including that these things cannot be measured by price, then they must reconcile themselves as much as possible with the wronged parties by making amends for the injuries they committed against them and by humbly asking for pardon. And we should make use of this manner of satisfaction, chiefly because of the harm and injury committed against a neighbor can never fully be recompensed. . . .

In every respect the same right (*Idem ius*) holds with respect to the treasures and precious objects found in the temples of idols, which in their unbelief and idolatry they honored as their gods, as do the objects they placed in their ancient tombs. For in the same way they did not consider them as abandoned objects nor did they renounce their property. Hence, not a single one of these objects, even after conversion, are unclaimed goods. Rather the goods have owners, or those who personally offered them to idols—whether they are living, or their heirs—which is in accordance with their laws and customs, corresponding to a right of inheritance.

If the Indians offered those objects to their false gods, they undoubtedly did so under a tacit proposal (*sub tacita conditione*): that their God or gods to which they made those offerings was believed to be the true God. As such, they were convinced that this was the true God given that the intention of gentiles tends principally and ultimately to worship the true God who can be known, albeit confusedly, by nature. . . .

It follows that the Indians offered things to others who were not gods supposing they were offering them to the true God to worship and honor him. Now afterward, by the grace of God, they

had received the faith and recognize they had been deceived to create those things. Evidently, they can regain and claim those things.
Even though they did not put those things there with sound mind,
believing in error that those idols were gods, they did so under a
tacit or implicit condition. If they were not considered true gods
or the true God, then there is no way they would have ever offered
it to others. Therefore, they have not lost their ownership of these
things (*dominium rerum*).

Document 21. "War of this kind is unjust": *The Only Way of
Attracting All Peoples to the True Religion*, ca. 1534

This document[5] is an excerpt from *The Only Way*, and it offers Las Casas's earliest and most concise critique of the Spanish conquests according to the just war tradition. The teaching on just war familiar to Las Casas
had its roots in classical Roman thought and was later developed by ancient and medieval Christian thinkers from Augustine to Thomas Aquinas.[6] Notice how Las Casas makes the language of right(s) central to his
account of justice. Are the ideas of justice as "right relationship" and justice as "personal rights" synonymous? On what basis does he claim that the
Spanish conquests were patently unjust? What is the link between love
and justice? How does Las Casas expand the scope of responsibility to address unjust war?

No war is just unless it is based on a cause that can be declared.
Certainly, any nation has a right against anyone who has provoked
it, because of an injury, which was caused by another nation. But
the infidel nations, living in their own lands outside of Christian
boundaries, are being subdued through attack in war by Christians
with no other title than making them subject to Christian rule
first in order to be disposed to receive the Christian religion and so
that obstacles to the faith can be removed. But no injury was made
against Christians by which to wage a right of war. Therefore, no
cause exists for declaring war against them.

. . . It is not by war, but by peace, benevolence, gentleness, kindness, persuasion, and the most intimate heart of love that leads
peoples, who have not yet been called, toward faith and religion.
Therefore, the cause for this war is dispelled. A war of this kind is
unjust.

Justice brings a certain rightness of order and governs the act of
a person according to a right relationship toward other persons, as

is shown in Book 5 of (Aristotle's) *Ethics*. The war of which we just referred is disproportionate with respect to infidel peoples. Those who attack by war and conquer without a cause have inflicted so many wrongdoings, harms, injuries, and irreparable damage to them deserving of no punishment. Consequently, this war is extremely unjust.

One of the precepts of justice is to do no harm to another (*Digest*, 1,1,10; and the *Institutes*, 1,1,1). But those making such wars on peoples inflict the most serious, immeasurable, unimaginable, and irreparable injuries without justification. Therefore, war of this kind is unjust and itself condemned by natural justice.

Another precept of justice is to protect and render to each person his or her own right. But by a war of this kind they attack, seize, disturb, destroy, plunder, and lay waste all rights and every good in plain sight. The war is unjust and completely marked by iniquity.

. . . Among all human beings, nature itself has established the right of kinship (*ius cognationis*). Therefore, it is contrary to natural right and thus intrinsically wrong for one man to assault another, which is supported by Justinian's *Digest* (1,1,3). And indeed, this right of kinship among all human beings is so natural and confirmed by the precept of the Lord, which says: "Love one another as I have loved you" and "Love your neighbor as yourself" [John 13:34, 15:12, Matthew 19:19, 22:39; Mark 12:31–33; Luke 10:27; Romans 13:9; Galatians 5:14]. It can neither be renounced by pact nor by mutual consent (*Digest*, 2,14,34 and 38; and *Codex*, 8,47,6). This right is demonstrated and confirmed habitually through jurists. And with the aforementioned war this right is shattered; indeed, all rights are violated. Therefore, war of this kind is unjust and condemned by every right.

Another conclusion shows such a war is unjust because it damages piety in so much as it is directed toward God. Those who kill, slaughter, and scandalize, they damage divine piety and honor by diminishing and obstructing the increase of God which occurs from the propagation of the faith and the conversion of peoples. They also harm piety no less in reference to the Christian religion, which a lawyer calls our esteem and self-respect, that is, on account of our established reputation. They defile this reputation of the entire Christian community, which they incurably slander through abominable activities contrary to the Apostle's precept: "Avoid giving offense, whether to Jews or Greeks or the Church of God" [1 Corinthians 10:32], so as "not to find fault with our ministry"

[2 Corinthians 6:3]. It also says in the *Digest* (28,7,15): "For where any acts injure our piety, reputation, or self-respect, and, generally speaking, are contrary to good morals, it is held that we are unable to perform them." This is affirmed here; therefore, such a war is unjust.

Finally, it is tyrannical. First, that is because it is violent, cruel, lacking culpability and cause like the work of thieves, plunderers, and tyrants who have no right to do such wrongful and abominable things—actions which inflict the greatest plagues, anxieties, and calamities upon peoples. . . .

Second, they are themselves tyrants because they place their own good and temporal benefit before the common and universal good, that is, the divine honor, salvation, and countless spiritual and material lives of peoples and persons. From which it is shown that a government acquired by means of such a war is unjust, evil, tyrannical, and full of God's condemnation, and should in no way remain legitimate.

These things are also proven by the following corollaries. . . .

First corollary: Everyone who wages the aforementioned war and cooperates in whatever way by means of ordering, advising, helping, and supporting the cause to declare war against the infidels, commits a grave mortal sin.

Second corollary: All those previously noted, who have committed or will commit oppressive wars, according to the aforementioned modes of cooperation, are obligated, if they wish to be saved, to seek restitution for the harmed infidels. They must also make amends totally and in full, for all the damaged things, moveable and immoveable, which have been taken through such war.

Document 22. "Those peoples had never attacked, nor committed injury, nor war": *History of the Indies*, ca. 1550–1560

This document[7] presents Las Casas's general position on justifications for war from the perspective of injured innocent persons, rather than a European colonial power. War is horrible. It is not something abstract but demands close attention to concrete details and context. Nevertheless, there are universal principles for ascertaining its legitimacy, which belong to a longstanding just war tradition in Western political thought. Although Las Casas presents three legitimate rationales for Christians to wage war here, he goes on to make an unconventional point about the seizure and enslavement of Africans under the Portuguese conqueror Prince Henry of

Portugal.[8] His interpretation of this test case that marked the beginning of the African slave trade set the parameters for recognizing the injustice of the Spanish conquests described in the rest of the *History of the Indies*. What are the rationales or just causes of war according to Las Casas? How do they compare and contrast with modern and contemporary justifications for war? How were the Spanish justifications of conquest in the New World similar to the Portuguese justifications in Africa?

> In the following year of 1445, Prince Henry sent a ship, which arrived at the island of Arguim. The captain of the ship along with twelve men mounted a small boat headed for the mainland about two leagues from the island. Once they arrived at the mainland, they entered an estuary. When the tide became low, the boat came upon dry land. The native people saw them and came with 200 men. They killed the captain and seven of the twelve men in the company, the others escaped by swimming to safety. These native people were the first who justly killed the Portuguese because the latter had killed and unjustly seized as described above [see Document 7]. Therefore, no one who has human reason, much less anyone skilled in letters, would doubt that all the native peoples opposed to the Portuguese had just cause for war.
>
> The next year, 1446, Prince Henry sent three caravels and his brother, Don Pedro . . . to enter the River of Gold and to work toward the conversion of those barbaric peoples to the Christian faith. And if they did not receive baptism, to be amongst them with peace and good-will. . . . As it was, the natives neither wanted to receive the faith; nor did they understand in their own native tongue what was being said to them, nor to make peace and have good will with people who committed such irreparable evils and injuries against them. This response was done with justice and plenty of reason. Whoever has any sense knows and agrees with this.
>
> It should be noted here that it is unlawful for a Christian people to wage war, disturb, or commit the slightest harm against the person or even the possession of any infidel—whether a Moor, Arabian, Turk, Tartar, Indian, or whatever other group, law, or sect—unless they have one or all of the following three causes (no other justifications are warranted, any others outside of these that some invent are ridiculous and malicious, because they offer occasions or are given to justify stealing what belongs to another and conquering territories of other peoples). Otherwise, Christians commit the greatest

mortal sins, and they are obligated to restore what they have stolen and make amends for the injuries they have caused.

The *first reason* is if the infidels oppose, wage war against, or unsettle our Christian faith actually (*actualmente*) or customarily (*en hábito*), the latter of which is to say, they are always ready to offend us even though at the moment they do not do it, or because they are unable to or are waiting for the right moment and time to do so. The Turks and Moors of the Berber lands and of the East are examples of this, as we see and endure each day. There is no doubt concerning the cause of just war against them, not only in situations when they actually attack, but also when they cease doing so, because it is evidently due to the widespread experience of their intention to destroy us. This war of ours against them should not even be called "war," but rather, a legitimate defense according to natural right.

The *second reason*, which can be considered just with respect to our war against them, is if they *maliciously* persecute, hinder, or impede our Christian faith and Christian religion; or by killing worshipers and preachers *without legitimate cause*; or by using force for the purpose of getting Christians to renounce the faith, or by giving a reward for abandoning the Christian faith and accepting their religion. All of this belongs to the hindrance and persecution of our faith. No Christian doubts that this cause justifies war against whatever infidels. That is because we have an even greater obligation to defend and preserve our holy faith and religion and to remove any obstacles in its way than to defend our own lives and our earthly commonwealth. After all, we are obligated to love God more than everything in the world.

I use the term "maliciously" to mean if we have probable reason to think that they do this to destroy our faith and to spread their own. I say "without legitimate cause" because if infidels kill and persecute Christians due to wrongdoings and injuries that they unjustly received, and by this cause preachers to suffer (even though these preachers are without blame), it is not because they preach Christ, but because they are associated with people who have offended the infidels and therefore are not considered innocent. There is no difference with respect to the aim of the one or the other. Our war against them would still be unjust, just as it would be to blame, eradicate, punish, or fight against infidels who are merely defending themselves and their goods. For if these infidels kill clergy and reli-

gious dressed in secular clothes accompanying those who were trying to kill and rob them, or affront and harm them in some other
way, then it is clear that these things are neither blameworthy nor
punishable.

The *third reason* for a Christian society to wage a just war against
any infidels is, or would be, to stop them from unjustly seizing our
kingdoms or other possessions, while they have no wish to restore
or give them back to us. This cause is generally known by every
nation and authorized by the natural law as a basis for a just war of
one people against another, since every people and nation are obliged by the same natural law. First, that they have a basis for war
against another; and to discuss, reflect, and consider the reason they
have and the fault of the other people. . . .

Apply the aforementioned reasons to the most harmful deeds
of the Portuguese against those peoples, which were nothing more
than cruel wars, killings, enslavements, leading to the total destruction and annihilation of many villages (of peaceful people safe
in their homes), and the damnation of many souls whose eternal
rest was forfeited. Those peoples had never attacked, nor committed injury, nor war; neither did they ever harm or hinder the faith.
Furthermore, they held their lands in good faith because they
never took it, nor did any of their predecessors . . . and there is neither writing nor memory that the lands possessed by these peoples
were ever seized from the Church. Then with what reason or justice
could the Portuguese justify or excuse so many evils and grievances,
so many deaths and enslavements, so many scandals and the loss
of souls, as in those poor peoples, even if they were Moors? For no
other reason than they were infidels? Oh, certainly what a supreme
ignorance and condemnable blindness this was!

VII
Canon Lawyer and Advocate

The documents below emphasize the canon legal thought and advocacy of Las Casas before the Crown, the Spanish *encomenderos*, and the papacy. Like other late scholastic and early modern thinkers, Las Casas "was part of a general movement of adapting ecclesiological and canon law concepts to political theory."[1] In this section, particular attention is given to the canon legal principles of consent, toleration, and the limits of toleration as crucial instances of political theorizing about the Indies. This section also considers the advocacy of Las Casas as a churchman, especially under his duty as a bishop challenging the policies of other Christians, clergy, and even the pope.

Document 23. "Every single person has to give consent": *On the Treasures of Peru*, 1563

This document[2] from *On the Treasures of Peru* considers the important legal principle of free consent: *"Quod omnes tangit debet ab omnibus approbari"* (What touches all must be approved by all). Though originally derived from Roman private law, the maxim became a principle of Church governance identifying the legal relationship between ecclesiastical leaders in the Latin West. Las Casas creatively applied the principle to establish legal immunity of the natives against Spanish imperial claims based on the papal donation of Alexander VI. The principle of *quod omnes tangit* offered a universal legal norm for all Amerindians according to the axiom of liberty whereby their voluntary consent was required for there to be legitimate Spanish jurisdiction.[3] Is Las Casas's argument about a right of consent applicable in reality?

Does his openness to the possibility that the Amerindians might willingly consent to Spanish sovereignty make him a more benevolent imperialist, but an imperialist nonetheless? What makes free consent still politically relevant in current discussions of neocolonialism and decolonial thinking?

Whenever a free person and, greater yet, a free people or community is bound to accept some burden or pay some debt, and generally when it is a matter of some harm, especially to many, it is right that all whom the matter touches be summoned and their free consent obtained. Otherwise, what is accomplished has no validity.

. . . It is proper that all the kings and the peoples of those Indian nations should be summoned, and the consent of those free people be expected and preserved. But these people have never so much as offered consent freely, which is necessarily required. To obtain it from them, it is necessary to convince and attract them by good reasons, with gentleness, kindness, and solicitude.

It is known by the law (having been cited and summoned) that whatever activity touches all must be approved by all—principally shown in *De regula iuris*, Book 6 of *Decretals*: "*Quod omnes tangit.*" Evidently, all who suffer injury or have their rights stripped away or become harmed, to those "the power of consenting and opposing has been given by natural right, by divine and human right, to whomever" [Baldus, *Commentaria omnia*, 1.7.39]. This is understood, according to Pope Innocent IV (in his *Commentary on the Decretals*, X. 1.2.6) and all the canonists in general, in this way: when something is common to the many, not as a collective or even a single body, but as individuals or concerning each one's right; then, truly, it is necessary for individuals to know and to consent. Subsequently, what is done by the many has no validity unless everyone agrees to it whether together or separately, which is consistent with Innocent IV (Baldus, *Commentaria*, 8.3.11).

. . . It is evident that in this case, truly, everyone, however great— kings, lords, rulers, chiefs, and magistrates, heads of state and the people, but also the least among us and every individual—ought to be summoned. And every single person has to consent; otherwise, what has been accomplished to the contrary in act is not valid. Not even if a people approve and the city consents will they be able to rule against a single person who has not been summoned or consented. In a matter shared by all, from the many to the individual, the greatest favor is given to liberty (Bartolus, *Opera omnia*, 2.14.7; Justinian, *Codex*, 7.71.8). . . .

Free consent is required from everyone and must be obtained. When all or a single individual has a thing or a cause that affects them, there must be approval by every single person. Otherwise, undoubtedly, all that is done has no validity. Individual persons, besides everyone else giving consent, remain free from having to comply.

. . . Even if the majority freely accepts without any fear imposed, they act against liberty, which does not prejudice those who do not agree—that is, the remaining minority unwilling to consent. . . .

With respect to accepting our Spanish king as the universal ruler, this affects all those Indian nations—not only kings and rulers, the people, provinces, cities, municipalities, and territories, but truly, even every single individual person of each town, city, or territory. Indeed, every person placed under incredible burden and paying off such great debt will be ruined, or at least greatly diminished, regardless of whether or not our government conducts itself rightly or successfully towards them. Their own liberty—of their kings and rulers, as much as the peoples and individuals of the islands—is more likely to be lost completely than to be enjoyed to a small extent (which is more than certain due to what has happened and is happening now, just as the affairs that have occurred demonstrate). By offering submission, obedience, deference, and various royal duties, so then from it comes the greatest damage, because all of them have been injured and have had every right taken away. But since they are free, a power and faculty of consenting and resisting is bestowed on them by natural right.

Therefore, of the whole, from the greatest to the least, all peoples and individual persons are summoned, and out of them everyone's free consent must be sought after and obtained. But this freedom (or the kind necessarily required) anyhow, has never been respected, as is well known. Therefore, in order to obtain their free consent (*liber consensus*), it is necessary to do so with good reasons, and with gentle, kind, and sweeter methods of persuasion and attraction.

Document 24. "It is not my business to pass judgment on those outside": *In Defense of the Indians*, 1550–1552

This document[4] highlights the contentious issue at the Valladolid debate between Las Casas and Sepúlveda and Reformation Europe more broadly: religious coercion. Was it lawful for Spain to use war and conquest as an effective means of converting the Amerindians to Christianity? Sepúlveda answered in the affirmative, identifying idolatry as a crime punishable by a foreign power through war. The humanist gave full-fledged support to an imperial European mission of civilizing and converting the Amerindians. In direct opposition, Las Casas denied using war and conquest in the service of promoting true religion. The Dominican friar and bishop appealed to the medieval canon legal principle of toleration. This principle traditionally set limits on Christian jurisdiction of those "outside" the church community such as Jews and Muslims. According to the document, why does the use of coercion to convert someone contradict the teachings of the Gospel? How would Las Casas's idea of toleration compare and contrast with modern ideas of toleration in democratic societies?

The second proof that unbelievers do not belong to the competence of the Church is what Paul says in 1 Corinthians (5:12–13): "It is not my business to pass judgment on those outside. Of those who are inside, you can surely be the judges. But of those who are outside, God is the judge." All doctors, Greek or Latin, sacred or otherwise, interpret these words of Paul to mean that, as a rule, the Church cannot judge unbelievers who have never accepted the Christian faith.

The reason for this is that God, who is the Lord of all things, did not will to grant his Church the power of judgment over these persons but reserved judgment for himself. . . .

Furthermore, a third proof that the Church cannot punish unbelievers is this argument, which I submit, along with myself and all my other statements, to its correction. It is not the business of the Church to uproot idolatry by force or to punish idolaters, at least if they are not its subjects. Therefore, idolaters and unbelievers do not belong to the Church's competence . . .

As a rule, then, the Church cannot forcibly destroy idols before pagans hear and freely embrace the truth of the gospel. For it is fatal to the spread of the true religion, unless the pagans possibly had a very strong inclination to embrace our religion or if they voluntarily subject themselves to our rule, for then the worship of idols could be prohibited by means of adding some slight laws, provided that any kind of scandal be avoided. This will occur but rarely, and only where the actual state of affairs shows that it will be to the advantage of the people. It is fitting that the worship of idols be dislodged not by the violence of men but by the word of God.

What would we do if, after the idols have been destroyed by

force, the pagans, still ignorant of Christ, would secretly offer their sacrifices to their gods in the mountain forests or in the deserts, where those who strenuously preach Christ habitually discover them? The idols may be taken away from the temples but not from their hearts. For this reason Gregory says very appropriately: "We destroy in vain all the ceremonies of unbelievers or [in vain] make rules as to how they should practice religion if thereby we cannot win them" [Gregory the Great, *Qui sincera*, cited in D. 45, c.3]. And so, Augustine says, let us first "break the idols in their hearts" [*De Verbis Domini*, Sermone 6, *de Puero Centurionis*]. Without the preaching of the gospel and the knowledge of the true God, idolatry will be abolished either late or never, according to Chrysostom and William of Paris (St. John Chrysostom, Homily 7 *In Epist. 2 ad Corinth.*; William of Auvergne, *De Legibus*, c. 28). Hence Saint Thomas teaches that the rites of pagans ought to be tolerated by the Church so that, when they hear the preaching of the gospel, they might be converted to the faith (ST II-II 10.11). He is speaking about pagan rites that are performed in the territories of the Church, since it would be pointless to say of others that they should be tolerated. The Church is concerned only with persuading men to abandon them by an appropriate teaching of the gospel. . . . Saint Thomas says:

> To avoid some evil, namely, scandal or discord (which could result from interference by the Church) or an obstacle to the salvation of those who, by being tolerated in this way, would be gradually converted to the faith, for this reason, whenever there has been a great number of unbelievers, the Church as even tolerated the rites of pagans and heretics. (Thomas Aquinas, *Summa theolgiae*, II–II 10.11)

Indeed, these matters are so clear that I think they will satisfy Sepúlveda, no matter how stubbornly he holds to this opinion. For why is it that he now commits slander? He even cites Saint Thomas against himself. Surely that saint wants pagans to be tolerated and to be attracted to the faith, not to be compelled by violence. To teach is Christian, to compel is tyrannical.

A general argument can be drawn from all the foregoing. Because nature itself teaches that every race of man must worship God and because divine worship is made up of ceremonies, it follows that, just as men cannot live without the true God or a false god believed to be true, they cannot live without the exercise of some ceremonies, especially since the common opinion among the gentiles has been that the whole status of a country is preserved in happiness by means of ceremonies and sacrifices. Therefore, if against their wills we should completely abolish their ceremonies, they would have, in addition to the great number of other resulting abuses, only an apparent adherence to the Catholic faith and the Christian religion, and we would appear to be openly compelling them to embrace that faith—and this is forbidden.

But when has there been such a multitude of unbelievers throughout the whole world as to constitute a just cause for tolerating their rites if they were subjects of the Church? Or in what other nations could idols be more easily destroyed in hearts, and idolatry thereby totally abolished and the worst scandals avoided, as well as the loss of innumerable souls if they were taught little by little and tolerated, than in our peoples of the Indies? Certainly, the holy Church itself knows quite well that it is not its concern to destroy idols and idolatry among the unbelievers about whom we are speaking, but only the divine word and the mild urging of reason, just as it has known how to use it from its very beginnings and will continue to use it (I hope) until the coming of the just judge and spouse, Jesus Christ.

Therefore, they who do the contrary, or claim that the contrary should be done, go against both the custom of the Church and the teaching of the holy fathers and the examples they set and believed. And so, finally, it is evident in this regard that they do not belong to the authority or jurisdiction of the Church.

Document 25. "Help to the oppressed against their oppressors": On the Treasures of Peru, 1563

This brief but essential passage from On the Treasures of Peru[5] considers the limits of toleration on the controversial issue of human sacrifice.[6] When Spanish sympathizers of the conquests like Sepúlveda surveyed the larger civilizations of the Incas and Aztecs, they pointed to human sacrifice and cannibalism as signs of cultural decadence. Moreover, they often made a humanitarian argument for war and conquest on the basis of protecting innocent civilians from oppressive and unjust rulers. Notably, Las Casas does support the use of force for the sake of humanitarian intervention but under strict prudential constraints. What moral principles does he apply to analyze the legitimacy of intervention? What is the role of religion in this case? Should humanitarian intervention be considered a moral cover for imperial expansion? Why or why not?

> With respect to the inhabitants of that [New] World, who have not yet accepted the Christian faith . . . it does not fall upon the Royal Highness to be concerned with their sins—no matter how serious, or idolatrous, or unnatural—that they commit or have committed within the boundaries of their unbelief and jurisdiction. However, they are to provide for them, as carefully as possible, through the teaching and examples of good men, who perform deeds more than instruct, thus illuminating them and leading them to Christ with the assistance of divine grace if only they are willing to hear the word of life voluntarily. But if the infidels are unwilling, they cannot be compelled to listen, and instead we should shake the dust from our feet upon them, like the form of preaching that Christ had appointed and commanded in the Gospel. For this was the way that Christ advanced and the form that was used by Him and His true disciples. . . .
>
> If, by chance, it comes to the knowledge of our kings that some of these infidels kill innocent persons to sacrifice them to their gods, or to consume their flesh—that is, when cannibals kill them for the purpose of feeding on human cadavers—then the Crown must attempt, with every possible peaceful means, to persuade them with gentle words and examples, again and again. This excludes cases of those who feed on cadavers of the dead due to smell or those offered who are prisoners of war, in which case the Crown has no jurisdiction over those who are outside. But in the alleged case, the Crown must insistently persuade them to abandon such practices in a gradual way.
>
> Now, if those unbelievers stubbornly refuse to abandon such practices, moderate force can be used to stop them. Yet it is not precisely for the reason of punishing such crimes, nor to make them slaves, because this case cannot be treated appropriately by war. It is instead a kind of defense. In this way, our kings act like private persons who offer help to the oppressed against their oppressors. In effect, by lacking power and jurisdiction, which our kings only have in potential (not actual) form, and even then, only in a limited sense, referring especially to those unbelievers who have never accepted the faith . . . our kings cannot punish them. To reiterate, we have nothing to do with the crimes that infidels commit in their unbelief and under their jurisdiction (as St. Paul affirms in 1 Corinthi-

ans 5:12). We can only take care to offer help to the oppressed and liberate those who suffer injury, just as we have extensively shown in *De unico vocationis modo* (Book II) and in the first part of the *Apologia*, which we wrote in both Spanish and Latin.

Concerning this case [of intervention], there are two things that greatly demand the attention of our kings:

On the one hand, the justification for it under the pretext of the manner of the crimes, or on behalf of liberating the innocent from unjust death, are the doings of iniquitous men having incurable greed, who always look for occasions by pretending falsehoods about things which are not certain. They do this to the point of seeking the opportunity of plundering the goods of Indians and subjecting these persons under themselves, which they make every effort to do as tyrants and thieves up to this point in these lands of the West, quite frequently.

On the other hand, prior to any force being inflicted upon them, it must be pondered if the amount of innocent people (who have committed no such wrong) destroyed in a war advanced against them is greater than those spared from physical ruin, . . . In accordance with divine precept, we should certainly cease rescuing innocent persons in such a situation and overlook them, because such an act [of war] would be vicious. Otherwise, it would appear contrary to the norm of reason, which says that the lesser evil should be chosen. . . .

Without comparison, it is a lesser evil to permit some innocent persons to suffer and be killed unjustly because of idolatry and cannibalism, than for us to rescue them from an unjust death by means of cruel wars, which can be called and are considered crimes against humanity (*calamitas generis humani*)—the greatest slaughtering of human beings among whom thousands and thousands of innocent persons are getting massacred.

Document 26. "Those Indians whose rights I have defended till my death": Petition to His Holiness Pope Pius V, 1566

This document[7] presents a final letter of Las Casas to Pope Pius V in 1566, the last year of life, reaffirming the previous policy of Pope Paul III. It is very brief but clearly summarizes his persevering pro-Indian advocacy and the ongoing relevance of his writings such as *The Only Way* and the *Apologia*. Despite his unflinching commitments, the justification for war against nonbelievers to remove idolatry and bring about conversion still remains strong among the partisans of conquest. Las Casas appeals to the pope, the final safeguard to carry out the protective duty of bishops toward the poor and oppressed, who must renounce indifference and luxury at the expense of the impoverished natives. It is his last impassioned attempt to summon the Church and the papacy to exercise its power for good in the New World for the sake of truth, justice, and love. That is, to be a cause for hope rather than scandal in a colonial world marked by tyranny, injustice, and the demise of native cultures.

In the book that I sent to your Holiness, I have declared what things are necessary for the proper method of preaching the Gospel, and when it is lawful to wage war against nonbelievers. I hope to elaborate further. By the blood of our Redemption, I sincerely beseech you to require that my book be examined. And, if found right, approved by seal, so that the truth may not be hidden to the detriment and injury of the Church, as the time may come (it may already be at hand) in which God discloses our blemishes and our nakedness is shown to all nonbelieving peoples.

Many are the flatterers who in secret, like rabid and insatiable dogs, bark against the truth. I humbly beseech your Holiness to make a decree (or decretal) declaring excommunicated and anathema anyone who says either of the following: that war against infidels is just if waged in order to remove idolatry, or to make preaching the Gospel easier, especially in reference to those infidels who are neither injuring us now nor ever have in the past; or those who say the infidels are not true owners of their possessions; or those who affirm that the infidels are incapable of receiving the Gospel or eternal salvation, on the basis of their so-called rudeness or backwardness. In fact, that is not those Indians whose rights I have defended till my death, with great effort and labor, for the honor of God and Church. In my book, I have clearly shown that all these things are contrary to the rules (or canons) of the Church, the Gospel, and natural law. Even so, I will confirm it further, if necessary, because I have it thoroughly verified and corroborated.

Experience, the teacher of all things, confirms that in these times it is necessary to renew all the rules that command the bishops to take care of the poor and oppressed, afflicted men and widows, even to the point of shedding blood on behalf of them, according to the duty of natural and divine laws. I humbly beseech your Holiness, by the renewal of these rules, to order the bishops of the Indies under

holy obedience the following: to care for the natives who are oppressed by hard labor and tyranny (more than one can imagine),
carrying on their flimsy shoulders a heavy yoke and unbearable load,
which is against every divine law and natural right. Therefore, it is
necessary that your Holiness order the bishops to defend this cause,
becoming a wall of protection for them, even to the point of spilling their own blood, as they are obligated to do so according to
divine law.

Bishops openly and unjustly ignore the language of their subjects, nor do they attempt to learn it carefully. Therefore, I humbly
beseech your Holiness to order them to learn the language of their
sheep. Now, many terrible indignities occur before your Holiness
as a result of the bishops not learning the language of their
parishioners.

Such great scandal and no less detriment to our most holy religion stems from this new situation where bishops, priests, and
friars are getting rich and living large. Meanwhile, their recently converted subjects remain in such extreme poverty, and many of them
die every day in utter misery because of the tyranny, hunger, and
excessive labor. Therefore, I humbly beseech your Holiness to order
such ministers, in accordance with natural law and divine law, by
which they are obliged, to restore all the gold, silver, and precious
stones they have acquired, for they have taken it from human beings
who suffer extreme need and who today live in misery, with whom,
according to laws natural and divine, they are obligated to share
their possessions.

Appendix A
Brief Chronology

1484	Birth of Bartolomé de las Casas, Seville, Spain
1492–1493	The first voyage of discovery, Christopher Columbus
1493	Bull *Inter Caetera* of Pope Alexander VI
1502	Las Casas's first trip to the Indies
1511	Antonio Montesino's sermon, Santo Domingo
1512	Laws of Burgos
1514	Massacre at Caonao, Cuba, and Las Casas's prophetic call
1515	Las Casas returns to Spain
1516	*Memorial de remedios* to Cardinal Cisneros
1517	Las Casas's second trip to the Indies
1517	Las Casas with the Hieronomytes in Santo Domingo
1517	Las Casas returns to Spain
1519–1521	Conquest of Mexico by Hernán Cortés
1520	Las Casas's third trip to the Indies
1519–1522	Ferdinand Magellan circumnavigates the world
1520–1521	Venezuela (Cumaná) experiment
1522	Las Casas joins Dominican Order, Santo Domingo
1526–1531	In Puerto Plata, "long sleep"
1527	Las Casas begins to compose *History of the Indies*
1531–1533	Between Puerto Plata and Santo Domingo
1532–1534	Conquest of Peru by Francisco Pizarro
1533	Las Casas and Enriquillo
1534	Las Casas composes first draft of *The Only Way*
1535	Attempt to reach Peru, Las Casas
1535–1536	To Nicaragua, Las Casas

1536–1540	Las Casas in Guatemala and Mexico
1537	Pope Paul III's Bulls on American Indians
1540	Return to Spain, Las Casas
1542	Publication of New Laws for governing the Indies
1543	Las Casas appointed Bishop of Chiapa
1544	Fourth trip to the Indies, Las Casas
1544–1547	In Guatemala, New Spain
1545–1563	Council of Trent Meets
1547	Return to Spain, Las Casas
1550–1551	Debate between Las Casas and Ginés de Sepúlveda
1552	Las Casas publishes major tracts, Seville
1553–1561	Las Casas in Valladolid
1561–1566	Las Casas in Madrid
1566	Letter to Pope Pius V
1566	Las Casas dies in Madrid

Appendix B
Some Questions for Consideration

- What is a "just" war? How did Las Casas contribute to thinking about war?
- How did Christians reconcile the use of force in proselytizing American Indians?
- What are some of Las Casas's arguments for the "only way" to evangelize among pagans and barbarians?
- How are some of the "modern" concepts of self-determination and human rights traceable to Las Casas's writings and positions in the sixteenth century?
- What is the role of history in the quest for justice?
- What are some of the principal elements of the "Black Legend," largely documented by Las Casas?
- How did Las Casas compare Indian civilizations of the Americas to other civilizations? To Spain itself?
- Describe Las Casas's changing views on African slavery.
- What role did Las Casas play in the discovery of America by Christopher Columbus?
- In what ways did Las Casas agree and disagree with the thought of the ancient Greek philosopher Aristotle?
- Was Las Casas a Christian imperialist? Why or why not?
- How does the ongoing dialogue on the narrative of possession rely on Las Casas's writings and perspectives?

Notes

Introduction

1. For the controversy surrounding Las Casas's birthdate, see Helen Rand Paris and Harold E. Weidman, "The Correct Birthdate of Bartolomé De Las Casas," *Hispanic American Historical Review* 56, no. 3 (1976): 385–403.

2. The term "Amerindian" is a conflation of "American" and "Indian" and employed to designate Amerindian peoples of the so-called "West Indies," distinguished from the inhabitants of the subcontinent of India. It is preferable to speak of native Americans as they knew themselves, to wit, Taíno, Nahua, Inca, etc., but often we refer to the entirety of the population, and so Amerindian is a useful term. "Indigenous" is also used for Amerindian in some historical literature, although that concept has broader application.

3. Jonathan Boyarin, *The Unconverted Self: Jews, Indians, and the Identity of Christian Europe* (Chicago: University of Chicago Press, 2009).

4. Matthew Restall, *Seven Myths of the Spanish Conquest* (Oxford: Oxford University Press, 2003), chap. 3; Ida Altman, *Contesting Conquest: Indigenous Perspectives on the Spanish Occupation of Nueva Galicia, 1524–1545* (University Park: Pennsylvania State University Press, 2017).

5. Bernal Díaz del Castillo, *The History of the Conquest of New Spain* (1632).

6. Francisco López de Gómara, *Historia General de las Indias* (Lima: Comisión Nacional del V Centenario del Descubrimiento de América Encuentro de Dos Mundos, 1993).

7. *Las Siete Partidas*, ed. Robert I. Burns, S.J., vol. 2 (Philadelphia: University of Pennsylvania Press, 2001), II, Title 23, Law II, p. 440.

8. Mario Góngora, *Studies in the Colonial History of Spanish America*, trans. Richard Southern (New York: Cambridge University Press, 1975), 132.

9. Cited in Kathleen Deagan and José María Cruxent, *Columbus's Outpost among the Taínos: Spain and America at La Isabela, 1493–1498* (New Haven, CT: Yale University Press, 2002), 16.

10. Andrés Reséndez, *The Other Slavery: The Uncovered Story of Indian Enslavement in America* (Boston: Houghton Mifflin Harcourt, 2016), chap. 1.

11. This and other subsequent quotes are from one of two editions of the *Historia de las Indias*. This citation is to Bartolomé de Las Casas, *Historia general de las Indias*, introduction by Lewis Hanke, transcription and index by Agustín Millares Carlo, 3 vols. (Mexico City: Fondo de Cultura Económica, 1951), III, chap. 78 end, and chap. 79, as quoted in Parish and Sullivan, *Bartolomé de las Casas*, pp. 185ff. There is one other edition of the *Historia* that I have used as well. *Historia de las Indias* forms volumes 3, 4, and 5 of *Fray Bartolomé de las Casas, Obras completas [Complete Works]* (Madrid: Alianza Editorial, 1989–1995). This edition is devoted to Las Casas's full body of works and comprises fourteen volumes. It is heavily annotated with extensive introductions to many of his works and is authoritative and as near to "complete" as we are ever likely to get. It was prepared by his fellow Dominicans through the Fundación "Instituto Bartolomé de las Casas," de los Dominicos de Andalucía. The overall director was Doctor Paulino Castañeda Delgado.

12. Bartolomé de las Casas, *An Account, Much Abbreviated, of the Destruction of the Indies*, ed. Franklin Knight, trans. Andrew Hurley (Indianapolis: Hackett, 2003), p. 23.

13. Peggy Liss, *Isabel the Queen, Life and Times* (New York: Oxford University Press, 1992), p. 217.

14. Casas, *An Account... of the Destruction of the Indies*, p. 50.

15. Paolo G. Carozza, "From Conquest to Constitutions: Retrieving a Latin American Tradition of the Idea of Human Rights," *Human Rights Quarterly* 25, no. 2 (2003): 292. See also David M. Lantigua, "Faith, Liberty, and the Defense of the Poor: Bishop Las Casas in the History of Human Rights" in *Christianity and Freedom, Volume 1: Historical Perspectives*, ed. Timothy Shah and Allen Hertzke (New York: Cambridge University Press, 2016), 176–209.

16. See, for example, Lewis Hanke, "The Sermons of Friar Antonio de Montesinos, 1511," in *The Spanish Struggle for Justice in the Conquest of America* (Boston: Little, Brown, 1965), pp. 17–18.

17. Cited in Gustavo Gutiérrez, *Las Casas: In Search of the Poor of Jesus Christ*, translated by Robert R. Barr (Maryknoll, NY: Orbis Books, 1993), p. 229. Originally published as *En busca de los pobres de Jesucristo* (Lima, Peru: Instituto Bartolomé de las Casas and Centro de Estudios y Publicaciones, 1992).

18. Casas, *An Account... of the Destruction of the Indies*, p. 36.

19. Daniel Castro, *Another Face of Empire: Bartolomé de Las Casas, Indigenous Rights, and Ecclesiastical Imperialism* (Durham, NC: Duke University Press, 2007).

20. Diego von Vacano, *The Color of Citizenship: Race, Modernity, and Latin American/Hispanic Political Thought* (New York: Oxford University Press, 2012).

21. Tzvetan Todorov, *The Conquest of America: The Question of the Other*, trans. Richard Howard (New York: Harper & Row, 1984), 185–93.

22. See the exemplary studies of Gutiérrez, *Las Casas*; David Lupher, *Romans in a New World: Classical Models in Sixteenth-Century Spanish America* (Ann Arbor: University of Michigan Press, 2003); Luis N. Rivera, *A Violent Evangelism: The Political and Religious Conquest of the Americas* (Louisville: Westminster/John Knox Press, 1992).

23. Rolena Adorno, *The Polemics of Possession in Spanish America* (New Haven, CT: Yale University Press, 2007), 63–64.

24. Bartolomé de las Casas, *Obras completas*, from vol. III of the *Historia de las Indias*. Included in *Obras completas* as vol. 5 of 14 (Alianza Editorial: Madrid, 1994), p. 2464.

25. *Historia de las Indias*, III, chaps. 3, 79.

26. Aristotle, *The Politics*, trans. Carnes Lord (Chicago: University of Chicago Press, 1984), Book 1, Chapters 2, 5, 13.

27. Helen Rand Parish, ed., *Bartolomé de las Casas, The Only Way*, trans. Francis Patrick Sullivan (Mahwah, NJ: Paulist Press, 1992), p. 34.

28. Ibid., p. 36.

29. Ibid.

30. Parish, *The Only Way*, p. 4.

31. Ibid., p. 41.

32. See Henry Raup Wagner, with the collaboration of Helen Rand Parish, *The Life and Writings of Bartolomé de las Casas* (Albuquerque: University of New Mexico Press, 1967), "The New Laws," chap. 10, pp. 108ff for details.

33. Andrés Reséndez, *The Other Slavery*, pp. 46–48.

34. Parish, *The Only Way*, p. 41, suggests that "his friends impressed on him that by accepting the miter, he would automatically be free from the vow of obedience, and could then use the ecclesiastical arm to enforce the New Laws."

35. Ibid., p. 100.

36. David T. Orique, O.P., *To Heaven or Hell: Bartolomé de Las Casas's Confesionario* (University Park: Pennsylvania State University Press, 2018), pp. 73–108.

37. Ibid., pp. 82–83.

38. Wagner and Parish, *The Life and Writings*, pp. 166–68; Adorno, *Polemics of Possession*, pp. 75–76.

39. Wagner and Parish, *Life and Writings*, pp. 137–38.

40. Ibid., p. 137.

41. Lewis Hanke, *All Mankind is One: A Study of the Disputation between Bartolomé de las Casas and Juan Ginés de Sepúlveda in 1550 on the Intellectual and Religious Capacity of the American Indians* (DeKalb, IL: Northern Illinois University Press, 1974), p. 64. Another of Las Casas's modern biographers, Manuel Giménez Fernández, expressed the same conclusion: "His [Las Casas] experience in Central America convinced him that only the mendicant orders could convert the Indians, but only if such missionaries were numerous, carefully selected, and did not scandalize their neophytes by dissolute customs or by alliances with the

men who mistreated them," from Fernández, "…*Las Casas, a Biographical Sketch*," p. 107.

42. Bartolomé de las Casas, *In Defense of the Indians*, trans. and ed. Stafford Poole, C.M. (Dekalb, IL: Northern Illinois University Press, 1992), which is Poole's trusted rendition of the "Defense" in English.

43. Hanke, *All Mankind*, p. 68.

44. This summary is presented in *Complete Works*, 10, "Controversia entre Las Casas y Sepúlveda, Nota introductoria sobre el título y su contenido," by Lorenzo Galmés, O.P., pp. 97–193. Galmés (p. 98) has a very useful introduction to the Soto summary that most students turn to in lieu of reading the more massive and somewhat intimidating original treatises prepared by Las Casas and Sepúlveda during the "debate," which was, as Hanke noted, really a "controversy" that lasted many years.

45. Ibid.

46. Ibid., pp. 113–14.

47. Las Casas, *In Defense of the Indians*, chap. 57, p. 342.

48. David M. Lantigua, "The Image of God, Christian Rights Talk, and the School of Salamanca," *Journal of Law and Religion*, 31, no. 1 (February 2016): pp. 19–41.

49. Brian Tierney, *The Idea of Natural Rights: Studies on Natural Rights, Natural Law, and Church Law, 1150–1625* (Grand Rapids, MI: Eerdmans, 2001), p. 276.

50. In W. Eugene Shiels, *King and Church: The Rise and Fall of the Patronato Real* (Chicago: Loyola University Press, 1961), p. 81.

51. David Brading, *The First America: The Spanish Monarchy, Creole Patriots and the Liberal State, 1492–1867* (Cambridge: Cambridge University Press, 1993), 87.

52. Juan Ginés de Sepúlveda, *Aqui se contiene una disputa o contoversia*, in *Tratados de Fray Bartolomé de las Casas* I (Mexico: Fondo de Cultura Económica, 1965), Objeción séptima, 310–11.

53. Las Casas, *In Defense of the Indians*, chaps. 38, 44.

54. Roger Ruston, *Human Rights and the Image of God* (London: SCM Press, 2004), p. 161.

55. For this last section, we wove elements covered in Wagner and Parish, *The Life and Writings*, pp. 184ff., Parish, *Bartolomé de las Casas: The Only Way*, pp. 48ff, and Giménez Fernández, "Las Casas, a Biographical Sketch," pp. 110ff.

56. Parish, "Bartolomé," p. 48.

57. There is some controversy over this log, which Helen Rand Parish, "Bartolomé," discusses on p. 48n74. Las Casas's copy of the log represents an historic preservation of one of the most fascinating and important documents in the history of exploration and discovery. See Oliver Dunn and James E. Kelley, eds. and trans., *The* Diario *of Christopher Columbus's First Voyage to America, 1492–1493*, abstracted by Fray Bartolomé de las Casas (Norman: University of Oklahoma Press, 1989), which views the history of the log rather differently from Parish.

58. For the newest introduction to this book see Bartolomé de las Casas, with

an introduction by Lawrence A. Clayton, *A Brief Account of the Destruction of the Indies* (Northport, AL: Regimen Books, Christian Classics, 2017).

59. For some studies of the Black Legend, see Charles Gibson, *The Black Legend: Anti-Spanish Attitudes in the Old World and the New* (New York: Knopf, 1971); William Maltby, *The Black Legend in England: The Development of Anti-Spanish Sentiment, 1558–1660* (Durham, NC: Duke University Press, 1971); and Jeremy Lawrance, *Spanish Conquest, Protestant Prejudice: Las Casas and the Black Legend* (Nottingham: Monographs in Post-conflict Cultures, 2009).

60. For a full discussion of this issue, see Parish and Sullivan, *Bartolomé de las Casas*, pp. 48ff, fn. 76, and Addendum III, "Las Casas's Condemnation of African Slavery," pp. 201ff.; also Lawrence A. Clayton, "Bartolomé de las Casas and the African Slave Trade," *History Compass* 7, no. 6 (2009): pp. 1526–41.

61. This incident described in Wagner and Parish, *The Life and Writings*, pp. 187–88, which draws upon Juan Antonio Llorente, *Histoire critique de L'Inquisition d'Espagne* (Paris, 1817), the latter printed in its original Spanish in Madrid in 1822, *Historia crítica de la Inquisición de España*, in ten volumes.

62. See Hanke, *All Mankind Is One*, pp. 117ff., for the continuing dispute with Sepúlveda through the 1550s.

63. *Lèse majesté* defined as the crime of violating majesty, an offense against the dignity of a reigning sovereign or against a state.

64. *Doce dudas*, in *Obras completas*, vol. 2, ed. Paulino Castañeda Delgado and Antonio García de Moral (Madrid: Alianza Editorial, 1992), pp. 70–71.

65. Wagner and Parish, *The Life and Writings*, p. 188.

66. Ibid.

67. Edward Cleary, *Mobilizing for Human Rights in Latin America* (Bloomfield, CT: Kumarian Press, 2007), p. 5.

68. José Martí, "El Padre Las Casas," in *La edad de oro* (Barcelona: Linkgua, 2008).

69. Gutiérrez, *Las Casas*, p. 44.

70. Gutiérrez, *Las Casas*, p. 206.

71. Alvaro Huerga, *Fray Bartolomé de las Casas*, vol. 1 (of 14 volumes) of *Obras completas*. Huerga's volume (vol. 1, the entire book) is entitled *Vidas y obras* and constitutes, essentially a self-standing biography (Alianza Editoria: Madrid, 1998), pp. 383–84.

Chapter 1

1. The best translation of Columbus's log of his first voyage is by Oliver Dunn and James E. Kelley, Jr., trans., *The Diario of Christopher Columbus's First Voyage to America, 1492–1493*, pp. 57–73. (Norman: University of Oklahoma Press, 1989). Half of this section—pp. 57–73—is the original Spanish, and two pages are copies of the original manuscript. The original is in the *Obras completas*, vol. 3, ed. Paulino Castañeda Delgado and Antonio García de Moral (Madrid: Alianza Editorial, 1988–90), between pp. 545 and 563, and also comprises a portion of vol-

ume 14 of the *Obras*, pp. 41–178, which includes the full journals of the First and Third Voyages.

2. The original is in the *Historia de las Indias*, vol. 1, pp. 332–34, ed. Agustín Millares Carlo (México: Fondo de Cultura Económica, 1965). Translated by the editors.

Chapter 2

1. The original is in the *Historia de las Indias*, in *Obras completas*, vol. 4, pp. 1335–39. Translated by the editors.

2. This selection is from *Bartolomé de las Casas, An Account, Much Abbreviated, of the Destruction of the Indies*, ed. Franklin Knight, trans. Andrew Hurley (Indianapolis: Hackett, 2003), pp. 18–21. The original is in the *Obras completas*, vol. 10, pp. 42–43.

3. This selection is from Knight and Hurley, *Bartolomé de las Casas, An Account, Much Abbreviated, of the Destruction of the Indies*, pp. 38–43. The original is in the *Obras completas*, vol. 10, pp. 54–57.

4. From "Las Casas' Prologue: The Lie Has Many Friends," in Sullivan, ed., *Indian Freedom*, pp. 14–16. The original is in the *Complete Works* (*Obras completas*), vol. 3, pp. 327–49. Sullivan excerpted from the long "Prologue," and we follow Sullivan's translation unless otherwise indicated.

5. This key quotation taken from the Spanish ("*de la relación verídica del hecho nace y tienen origen . . . el derecho*") has been retranslated by the editors in order to capture the moral importance of retelling history truthfully as a basis for legal reflection.

Chapter 3

1. In Parish, *Bartolomé de las Casas: The Only Way*, section entitled "Addendum III: Las Casas' Condemnation of African Slavery," pp. 201–208. The original is in the *Obras completas*, vol. 5, pp. 2189–94 and 2321–25 and vol. 3, pp. 468–475 (Parish extracted portions of each).

2. This version of the Montesino sermon is translated by the editors. The original is in the *Obras completas*, vol. 5, pp. 1761–65.

3. From Francis Patrick Sullivan, S.J., *Indian Freedom: The Cause of Bartolomé de las Casas, 1484–1566, A Reader*, Part 3, Creating Pro-Indian Law, section 3, "Selections from the New Laws of 1542." The original is in *Leyes y ordenanzas nuevamente hechas por S.M. para la gobernacion de las indias, y buen tratamiento de los indios*, in Joaquín García Icazbalceta, *Colección de documentos para la historia de México*, versión actualizada (Alicante: Biblioteca Virtual Miguel de Cervantes, 1999; publicación original, México: Antigua Librería, 1858–1866; notas de reproducción original: Edición digital basada en la edición de México: Antigua Librería, 1858–1866). In Biblioteca Virtual Miguel de Cervantes, http://www.cervantesvirtual.com/nd/ark:/59851/bmc4b2z9. We have followed some of Sul-

livan's translation, which is acceptable in the main, but retranslated all passages ourselves.

4. See Lawrence A. Clayton, *Bartolomé de las Casas: A Biography* (New York: Cambridge University Press, 2012), chap. 10, "The New Laws," pp. 270ff.

5. *Naboría* and *tapia* refer to the serf-like status of Indians providing lifelong personal service to their Spanish masters.

6. The original is in the *Obras completas*, vol. 10, pp. 326–31, as well as in *Tratados*, vol. 2, pp. 741–59. From Sullivan, *Indian Freedom*, section 2, "Twenty Reasons against the *Encomienda*," pp. 241–43.

Chapter 4

1. In *Obras completas*, vol. 5, pp. 2404–06, 2410–13, translated by the editors.

2. Las Casas is generally referring to the used and abused teaching of Aristotle from Book 1 of the *Politics* (1255a1–2), where the Philosopher indicates that some people are by nature free and others are by nature slaves. Aristotle's belief that Greeks should rule over barbarian others made this ancient teaching highly adaptable to European ethnic imperialism, as seen in this instance.

3. The original is in *Obras completas*, vol. 2, pp. 13–23.

4. *In Defense of the Indians*, trans. Stafford Poole (DeKalb, IL: Northern Illinois University Press, 1992), chap. 26, pp. 175–181.

Chapter 5

1. *Apologética historia sumaria II*, in *Obras completas*, vol. 7, pp. 536–38, translated by the editors.

2. Cary J. Nederman, *Worlds of Difference: European Discourses of Toleration, c. 1100–c.1550* (University Park: Pennsylvania State University Press, 2000), p. 101.

3. Cicero, *The Republic* and *The Laws*, trans. Niall Rudd (New York: Oxford University Press, 1998), 107–8.

4. This is a new translation by the editors of Pope Paul III's *Sublimis Deus* from the Latin, transcribed in *Las Casas en México*, ed. Helen Rand Parish and Harold Weidman (México: Fondo de Cultura Económica, 1992), pp. 310–11.

5. Parish, "Una historia desconocida," in *Las Casas en México*, p. 18.

6. Poole, *In Defense of the Indians*, chap. 3, pp. 37–40.

7. Ibid., chap. 4, pp. 41–49.

Chapter 6

1. *De regia potestate*, the original is in the *Obras completas*, vol. 12, pp. 35–165. Translated by the editors.

2. Half of the twelve pages are in Latin; the other half are in Spanish. We translate only two of the numerous "principles" of *Principia Quaedam*, pp. 1234–51 in *Tratados de Fray Bartolomé de las Casas* II. Translated by the editors.

3. Consider Deuteronomy 17:15, where the Lord instructed the Israelites: "You may indeed set over you a king whom the Lord your God will choose."

4. *De thesauris*, in *Obras completas*, vol. 11.1, pp. 17 and 61–63. Translated by the editors.

5. *De unico vocationis modo*, in *Obras completas*, vol. 2, pp. 497–501, 503, 523. Translated by the editors.

6. For a comprehensive overview of Western political thinkers belonging to the just war tradition from antiquity to today, consider *Just War Thinkers: From Cicero to the 21st Century*, ed. Daniel R. Brunstetter and Cian O'Driscoll (New York: Routledge, 2018). See, especially, the chapter on Las Casas by Brunstetter, pp. 92–104.

7. *Historia de las Indias*, ed. Millares Carlo, I, chap. 25, pp. 133–37. Translated by the editors.

8. Often referred to as Prince Henry the Navigator since he sponsored much of Portugal's voyages of exploration and discovery into the Canary Islands and Africa during the first half of the fifteenth century. Prince Henry was the leader of the Portuguese crusading knights known as the Order of Christ.

Chapter 7

1. Kenneth Pennington, "Bartolomé de Las Casas and the Tradition of Medieval Law," *Church History* 39, no. 2 (1970): p. 151.

2. *De thesauris*, in *Obras completas*, vol. 11.1, pp. 199–213. Translated by the editors.

3. José Cárdenas Bunsen, "Consent, Voluntary Jurisdiction and Native Political Agency in Bartolomé de Las Casas' Final Writings," *Bulletin of Spanish Studies* 91, no. 6 (2014): 793–817.

4. Poole, *In Defense of the Indians*, chap. 7, pp. 63–70.

5. *De thesauris*, in *Obras completas*, vol. 11.1, pp. 435–37. Translated by the editors.

6. For greater attention to Las Casas's controversial treatment of human sacrifice, see Sabine MacCormack, *Religion in the Andes: Vision and Imagination in Early Colonial Peru* (Princeton, NJ: Princeton University Press, 1991), chap. 5; David M. Lantigua, "Religion within the Limits of Natural Reason: The Case of Human Sacrifice," in *Bartolomé de las Casas, O.P.: History, Philosophy, and Theology in the Age of European Expansion*, ed. David T. Orique, O.P., and Rady Roldán-Figueroa (Leiden: Brill, 2019), 280–309; See also Gutiérrez, *Las Casas*, pp. 175–84.

7. The original is in the *Obras completas*, vol. 13, pp. 370–71. Translated by the editors.

Selected Bibliography

Adorno, Rolena. *The Polemics of Possession in Spanish American Narrative*. New Haven, CT: Yale University Press, 2007.

Brading, David. *The First America: The Spanish Monarchy, Creole Patriots and the Liberal State, 1492–1867*. Cambridge: Cambridge University Press, 1993.

Clayton, Lawrence A. *Bartolomé de las Casas: A Biography*. New York: Cambridge University Press, 2012.

Clayton, Lawrence A. *Bartolomé de las Casas and the Conquest of the Americas*. New York: Wiley Blackwell, 2011.

Friede, Juan, and Benjamin Keen, eds. *Bartolomé de las Casas in History: Toward an Understanding of the Man and His Work*. Dekalb, IL: Northern Illinois University Press, 1971.

Gutiérrez, Gustavo, O.P. *Las Casas: In Search of the Poor of Jesus Christ*. Translated by Robert R. Barr. Maryknoll, NY: Orbis Books, 1993.

Hanke, Lewis. *All Mankind Is One: A Study of the Disputation between Bartolomé de las Casas and Juan Ginés de Sepúlveda in 1550 on the Intellectual and Religious Capacity of the American Indians*. DeKalb, IL: Northern Illinois University Press, 1974.

Hanke, Lewis. *Aristotle and the American Indians: A Study in Race Prejudice in the Modern World*. Bloomington: Indiana University Press, 1959.

Hanke, Lewis. *The Spanish Struggle for Justice in the Conquest of America*. 1949. Dallas: Southern Methodist University Press, 2002.

Keen, Benjamin. *Essays in the Intellectual History of Colonial Latin America*. Boulder, CO: Westview Press, 1998.

Las Casas, Bartolomé de. *An Account, Much Abbreviated, of the Destruction of the Indies, with Related Texts*. Edited and with an introduction by Franklin W. Knight. Translated by Andrew Hurley. Indianapolis: Hackett Publishing, 2003.

Las Casas, Bartolomé de. *In Defense of the Indians*. Translated by Stafford Poole, C.M. Dekalb, IL: Northern Illinois University Press, 1992.

Lupher, David A. *Romans in a New World: Classical Models in Sixteenth-Century Spanish America*. Ann Arbor: University of Michigan Press, 2003.

MacCormack, Sabine. *Religion in the Andes: Vision and Imagination in Early Colonial Peru*. Princeton, NJ: Princeton University Press, 1991.

Orique, David T., O.P. *To Heaven or Hell: Bartolomé de Las Casas's Confesionario*. University Park: Pennsylvania State University Press, 2018.

Orique, David T., and Rady Roldán-Figueroa, eds. *Bartolomé de las Casas, O.P.: History, Philosophy, and Theology in the Age of European Expansion*. Leiden: Brill, 2019.

Parish, Helen Rand, ed. *Bartolomé de las Casas: The Only Way*. Translated by Francis Patrick Sullivan. Mahwah, NJ: Paulist Press, 1992.

Reséndez, Andrés. *The Other Slavery: The Uncovered Story of Indian Enslavement in America*. Boston: Houghton Mifflin Harcourt, 2016.

Restall, Matthew. *Seven Myths of the Spanish Conquest*. Oxford: Oxford University Press, 2003.

Rivera-Pagán, Luis N. *A Violent Evangelism: The Political and Religious Conquest of the Americas*. Louisville: Westminster/John Knox Press, 1992.

Sanderlin, George. *Bartolomé de las Casas: A Selection of His Writings*. New York: Alfred A. Knopf, 1971.

Sullivan, Francis Patrick, S.J. *Indian Freedom: The Cause of Bartolomé de las Casas. A Reader*. Kansas City: Sheed & Ward, 1995.

Todorov, Tzvetan. *The Conquest of America: The Question of the Other*. Translated by Richard Howard. New York: Harper & Row, 1984.

Wagner, Henry Raup, with the collaboration of Helen Rand Parish. *The Life and Writings of Bartolomé de las Casas*. Albuquerque: University of New Mexico Press, 1967.

Index